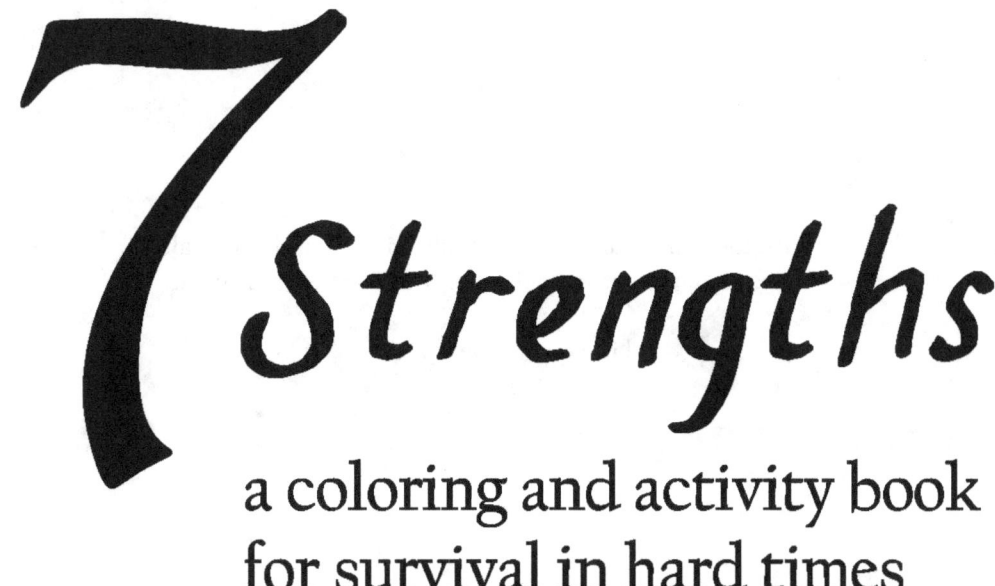

7 Strengths

a coloring and activity book for survival in hard times

by Rhea Ewing

With love and thanks to my family, friends, and above all my partner, who proofread and edited much of this book.

Liz, you are the loveliest.

How to use this book...

This book is structured around seven key concepts I've identified for my own strength and resiliency. Each section contains coloring pages, activities, exercises, and a brief explanation of the inspiration behind the images. I'd like to thank Joan Roughgarden for her book *Evolution's Rainbow,* which inspired a few key parts of this book.

Feel free to do the activities in order, flip to a random page, or skip anything that doesn't appeal to you. This is your book, after all!

If you're feeling social, you're welcome to share finished coloring pages with me by email or social media. You can send your files to rheaewing@gmail.com, or tag me @finecomic on twitter and tumblr or @rhea.ewing on instagram. I share these images with my followers and it's a delight to see different interpretations of my work.

In any case, I hope you enjoy this book. Thanks goes to my Patreon and Kickstarter supporters for making it happen!

Oh, and one more thing...

A word on advice...

Here's the thing about advice: what's good for me might be bad for you.

This book collects and summarizes my work on understanding my own keys to strength and resiliency. Yours are probably different! The things that allow me to live and work may be useless to you, or might even get in your way.

Instead of looking at this book as a prescribed toolset, I'd like you to look at this book as a way of thinking about the world and ourselves. This book is an invitation to notice the natural world and the diverse ways creatures have found to survive in it. We humans are also trying to survive and thrive, and our own need to find guidance, justification of our views, and a sense of kinship in the natural world shapes our view of it. This book asks you to observe both the world and yourself, find what lessons you can in each, and be willing to challenge your assumptions about both.

I hope the coloring pages in this book bring you a little peace, and I hope the exercises and activities provide you with a little bit of insight. Above all, I hope this book inspires you to connect with others and find your own points of strength and resiliency.

Thanks for being here.

-Rhea

Resiliency

How do you decide when to hold on and when to let go?

Tidal species live in a world of constant change. They must be able to survive being both in and out of the water and handle the never-ending waves crashing against them.

Barnacles are a type of crustacean. They hold themselves in place with a natural adhesive "cement" that they produce themselves. They are so steadfast and stubborn that there is an entire industry devoted to producing powerful solvents to remove them from ships and docks.

Many seaweed species take a different approach, embracing flexibility and flowing with the tides. Letting go of the idea of a set and stable form, they allow themselves to be pushed and pulled as conditions change. The seaweed here has small pockets of air, which allow it to float in the water.

Mussels close up tight when the tide is low to preserve themselves. When the tide rises again, they open and allow the water to flow through them, filtering out the nutrients they need to survive.

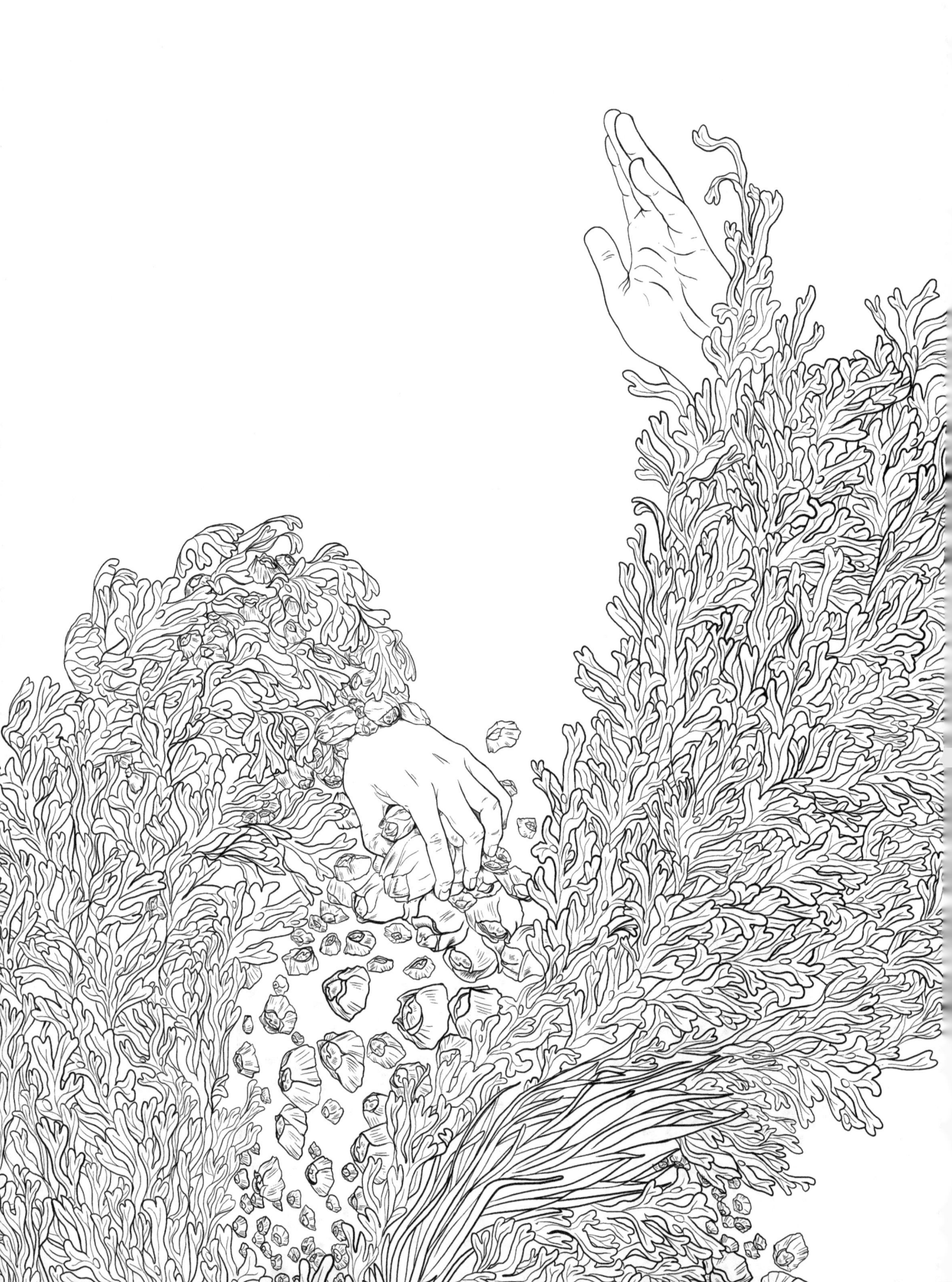

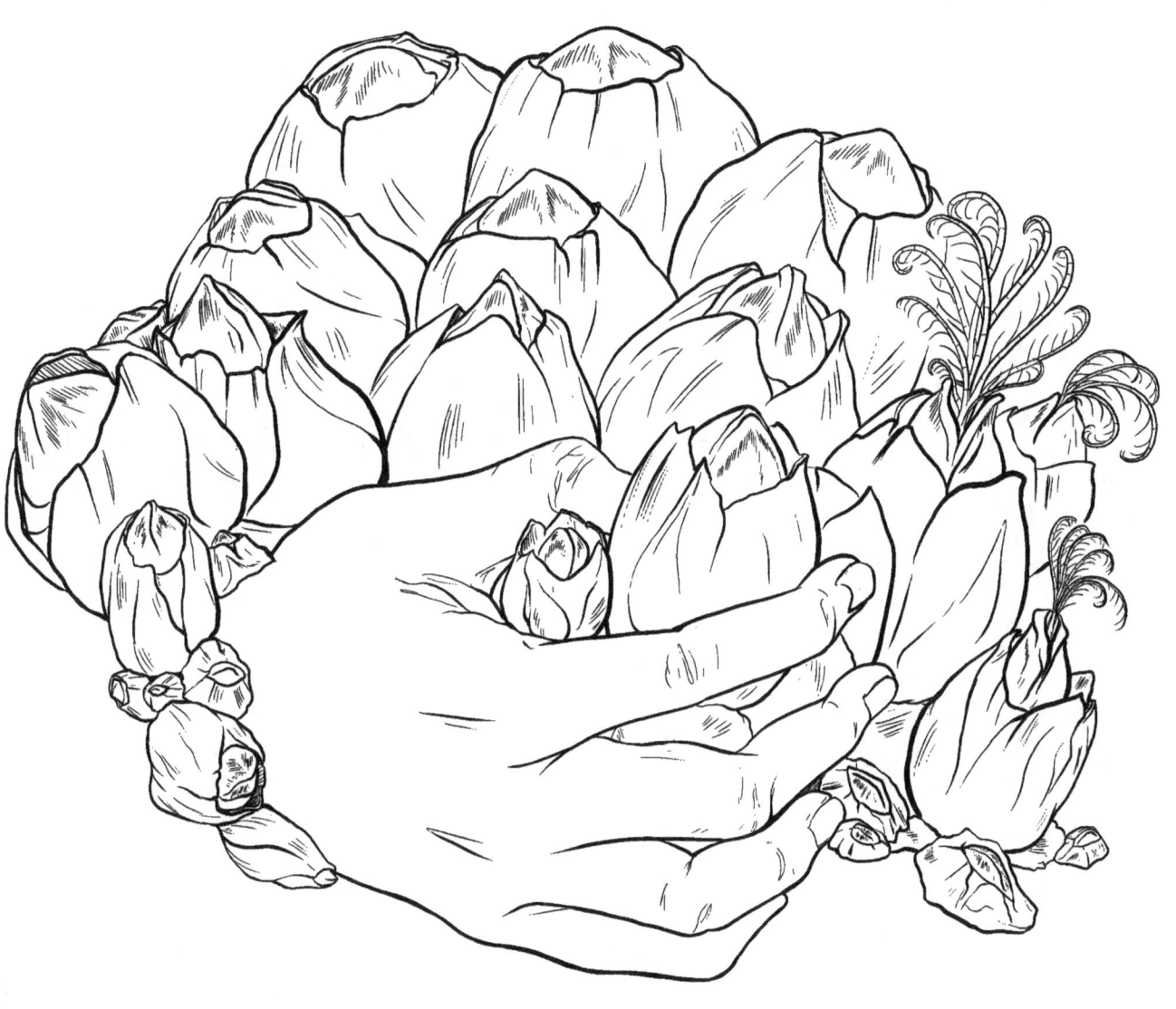

Hold Tight

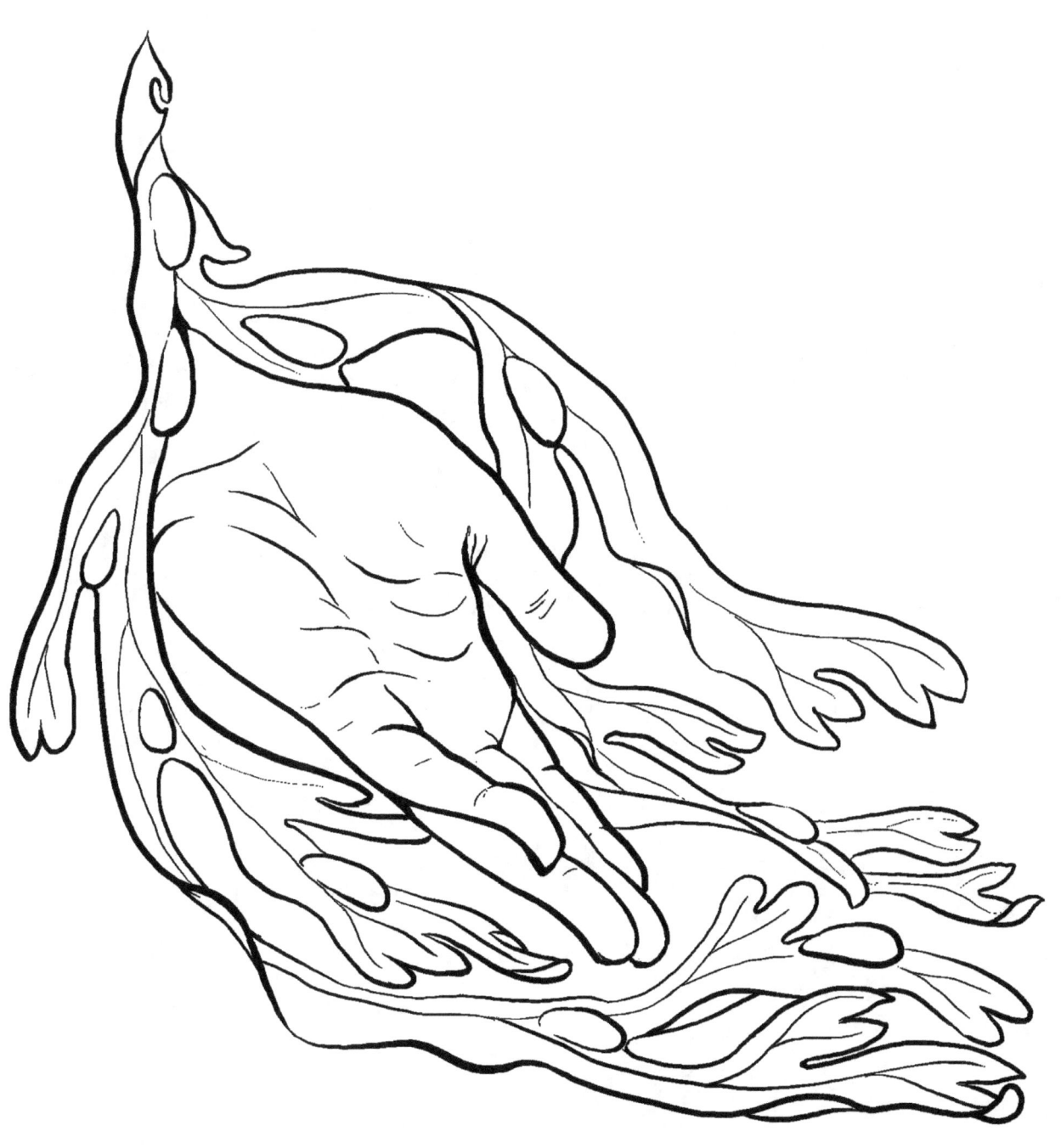

Let Go

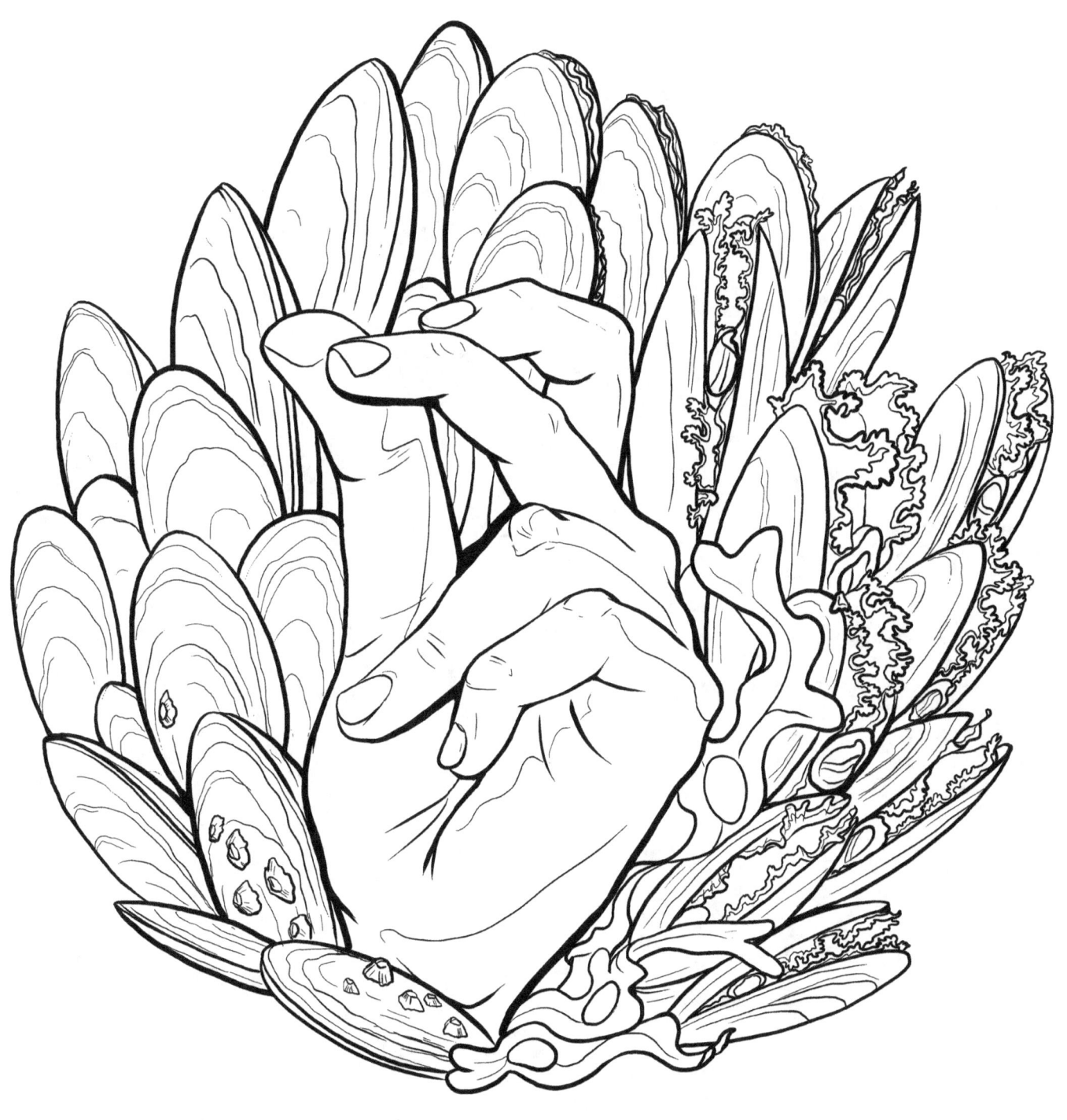

Adapt

Resiliency Activities

1. Choose something you have that you no longer need. Draw or write it down below. What can you do with it instead of holding on to it?

2. Now think of something you'd like to hold on to. Complete the sentence:

I am choosing to hold on to....

3. Welcoming new experiences is another aspect of resilience. Make a plan to do something new next week: learn a new skill, try a new food, or go somewhere you've never been before.

Hold Tight

Connect the dots
to encircle what's
worth holding on to.

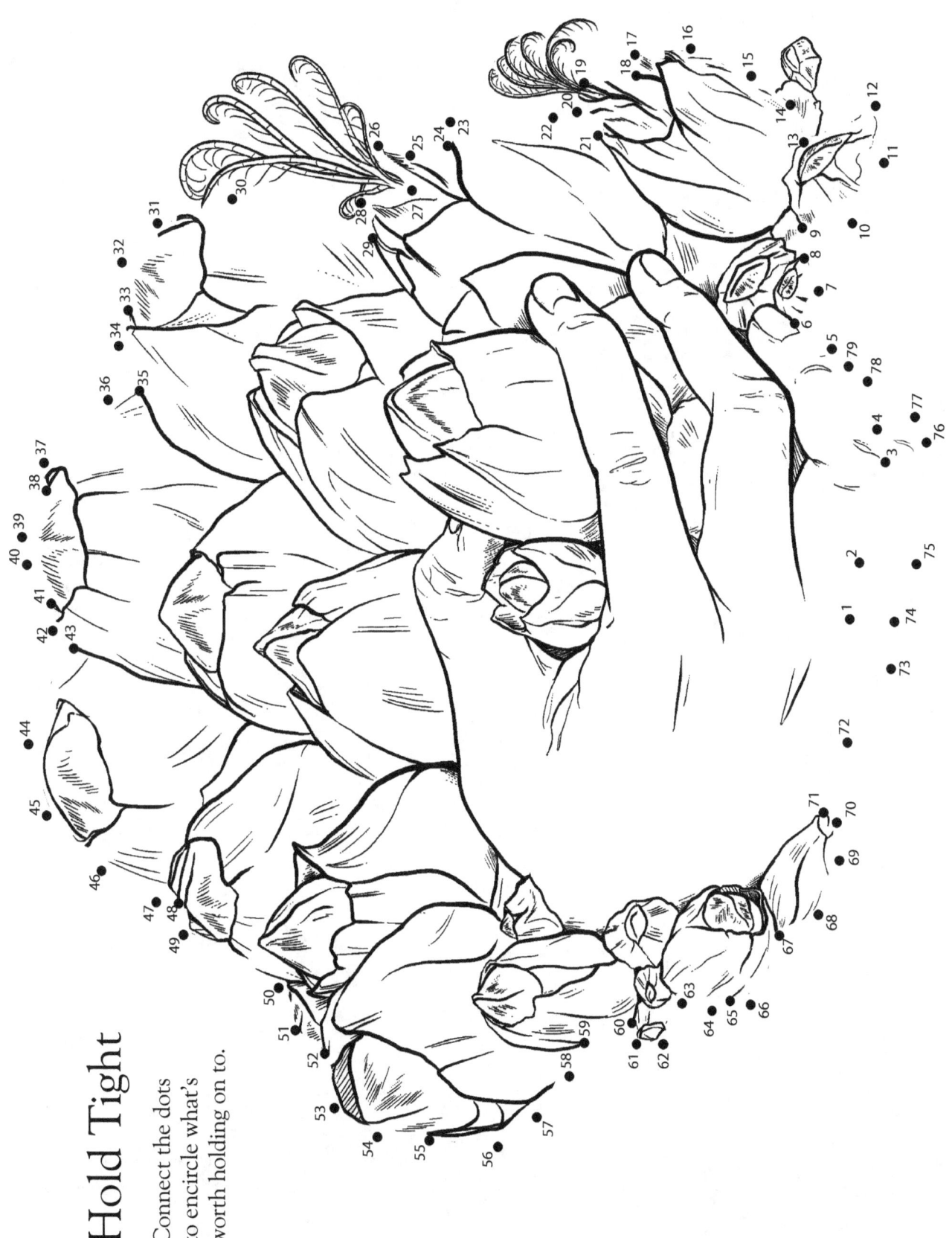

Let Go

Think of something you would like to let go of. Draw it here. If you are ready to let go, burn or recycle the drawing. If not, it is okay to hold on a little longer.

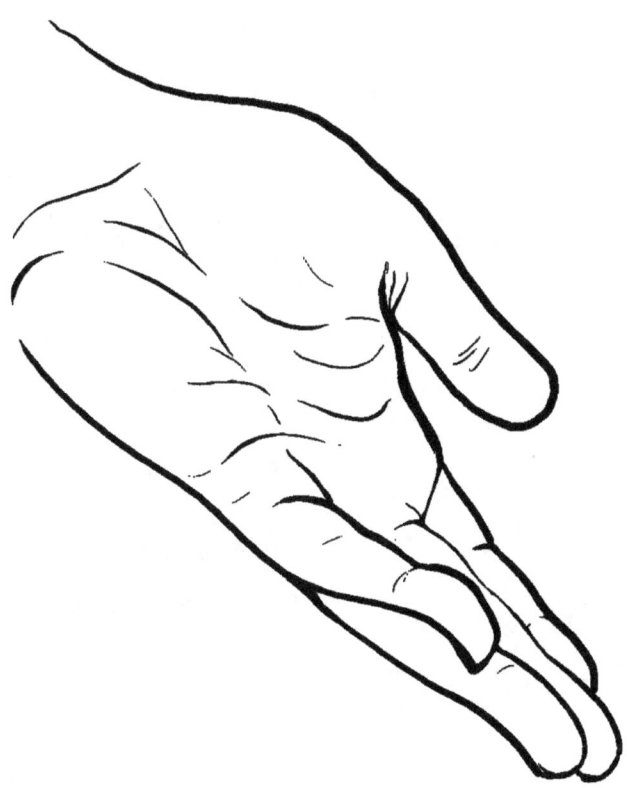

Adapt

Make one or more new drawings out of the lines below. If you get stuck, turn the page upside down for a new perspective.

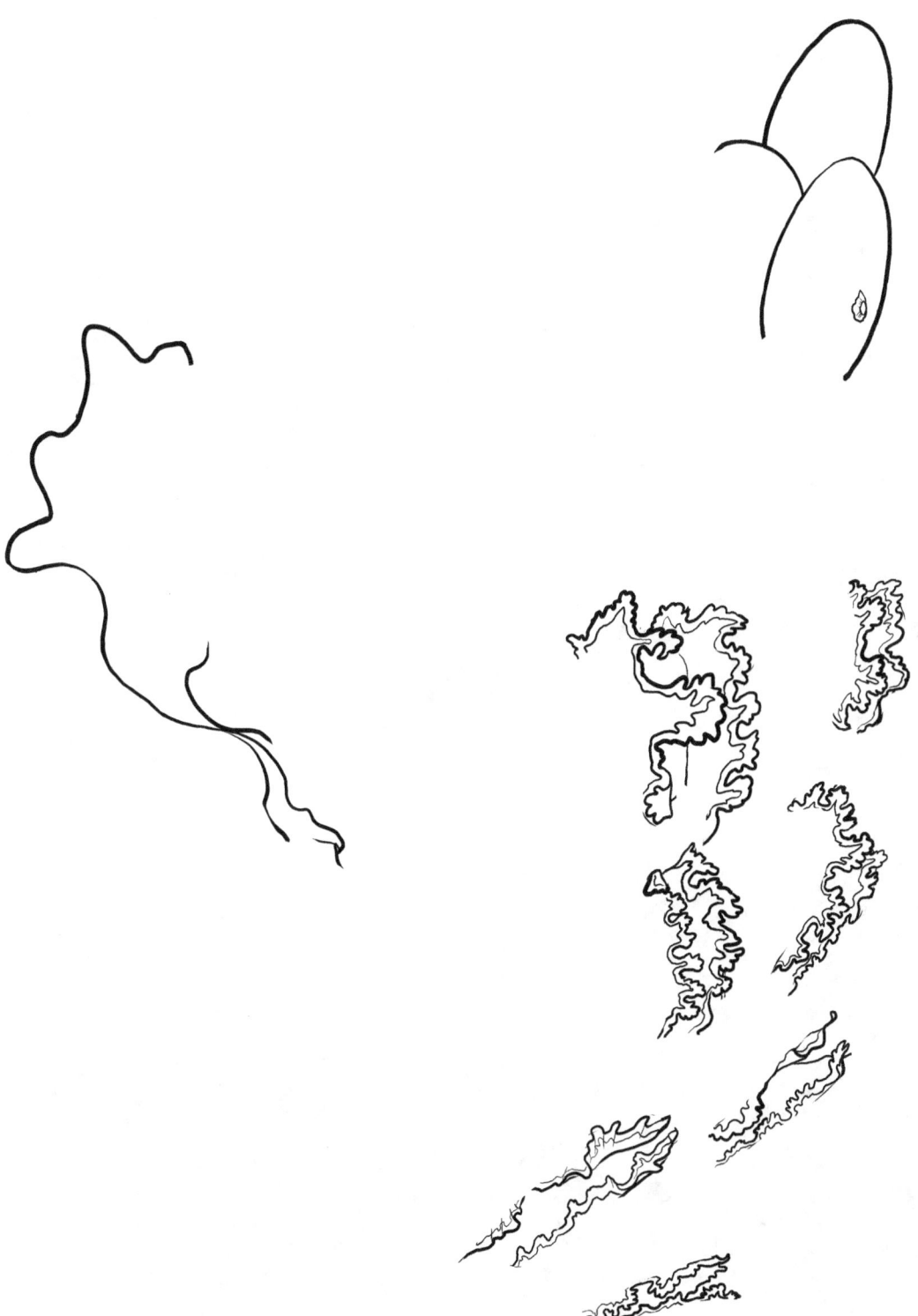

Flamboyancy

You are seen by others. What do you want them to know?

Bright colors in nature can act as a warning. The startling black and yellow stripes of a hornet and the bombastic colors of a nudibranch warn of painful stings. Many animals without stingers or other means of defense will mimic the bright colors of those that do—an effective defense mechanism in and of itself.

Plants and animals will also use bright colors to attract others towards them. Brilliant displays can be a promise of nectar, and invitation for courtship, or an advertisement of fitness and abundance. The brilliant colors and complex dance of a peacock spider allow him to court his mates with style.

Sometimes animals will draw attention to themselves merely for their own amusement. Crows will often tug on the tail feathers of larger birds of prey, then hop away as if nothing happened, confusing the larger bird. Sometimes this is a diversion technique to steal the other bird's meal—other times they seem to do it for no reason other than a good laugh.

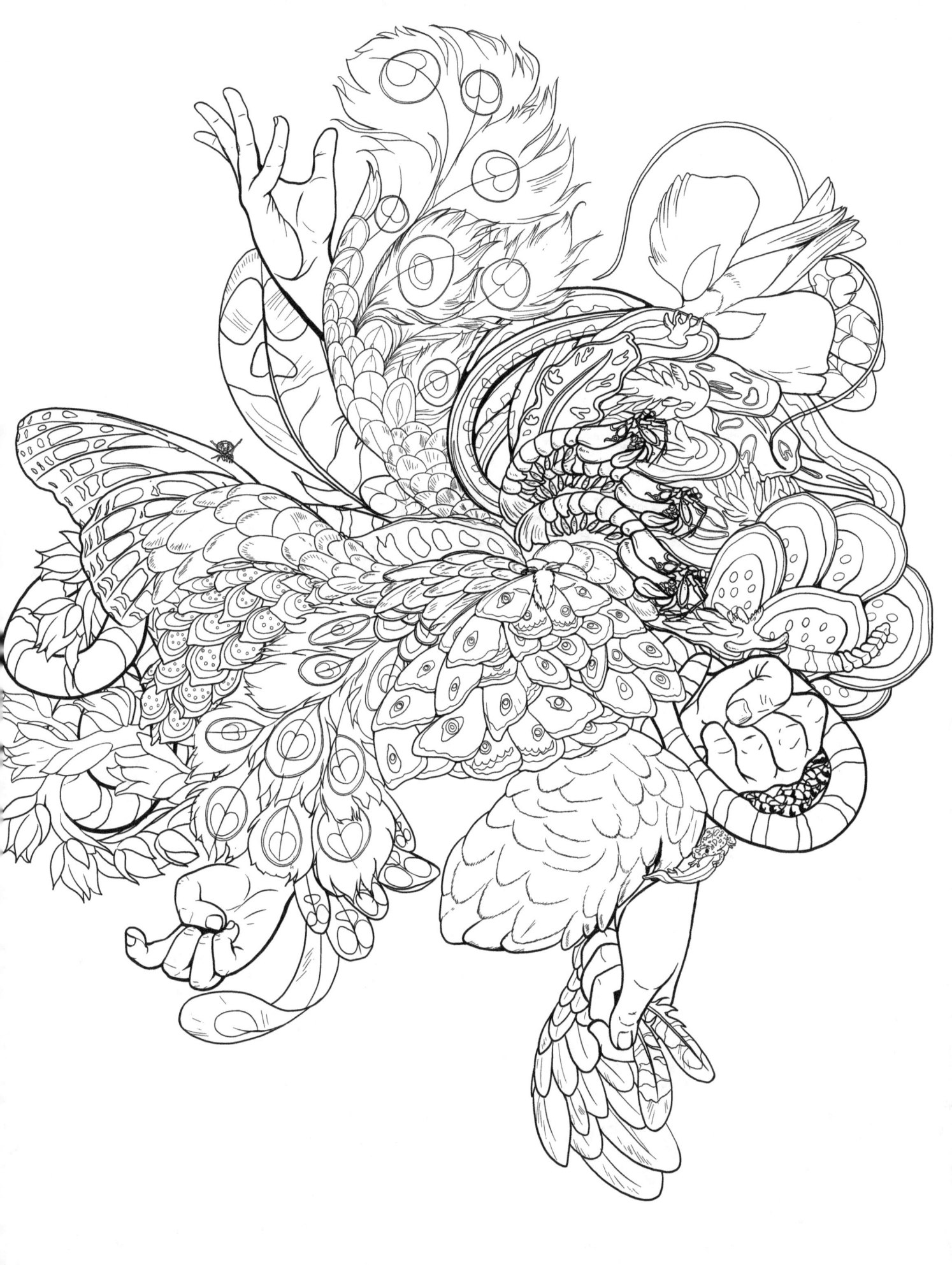

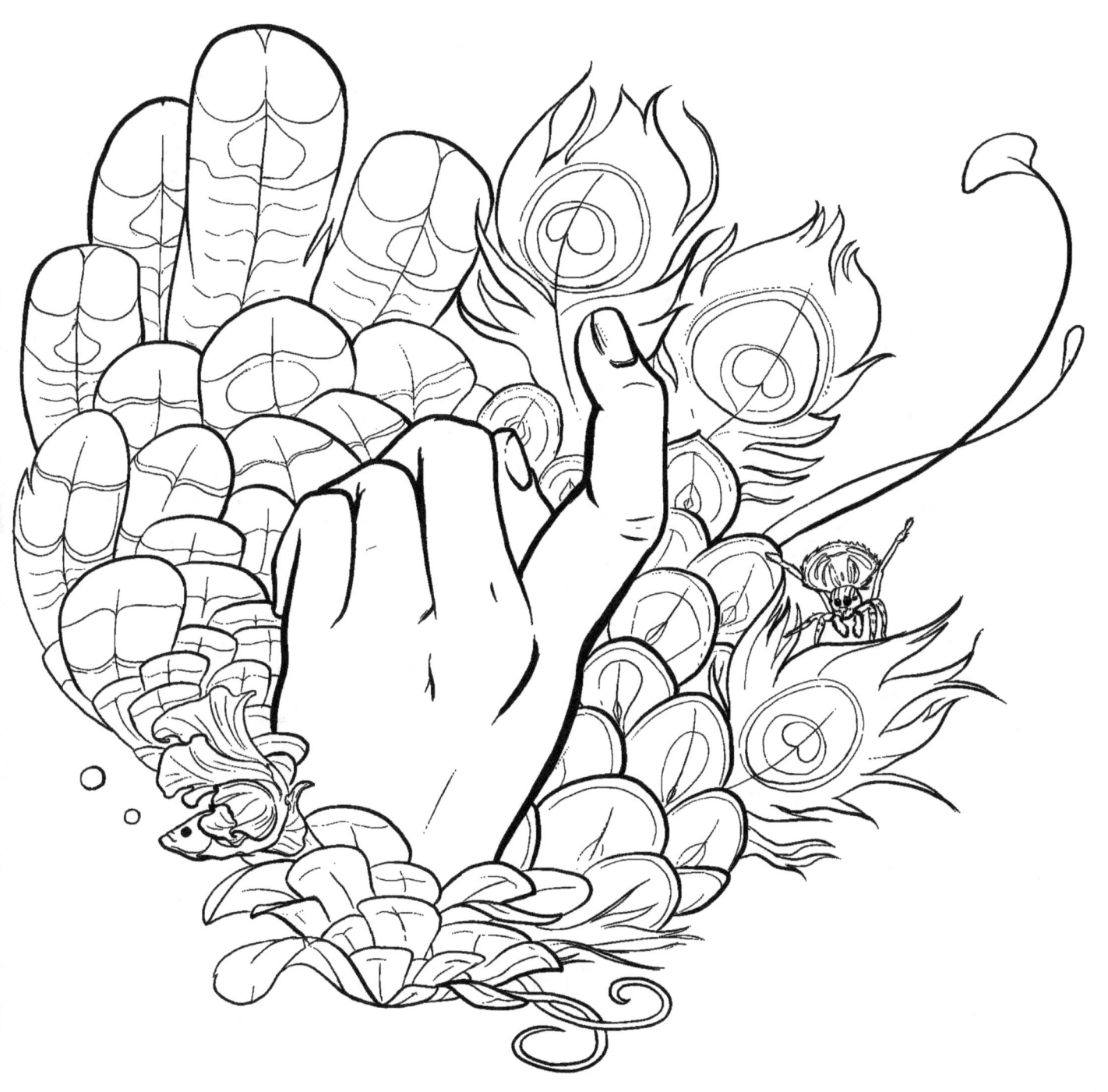

Attract

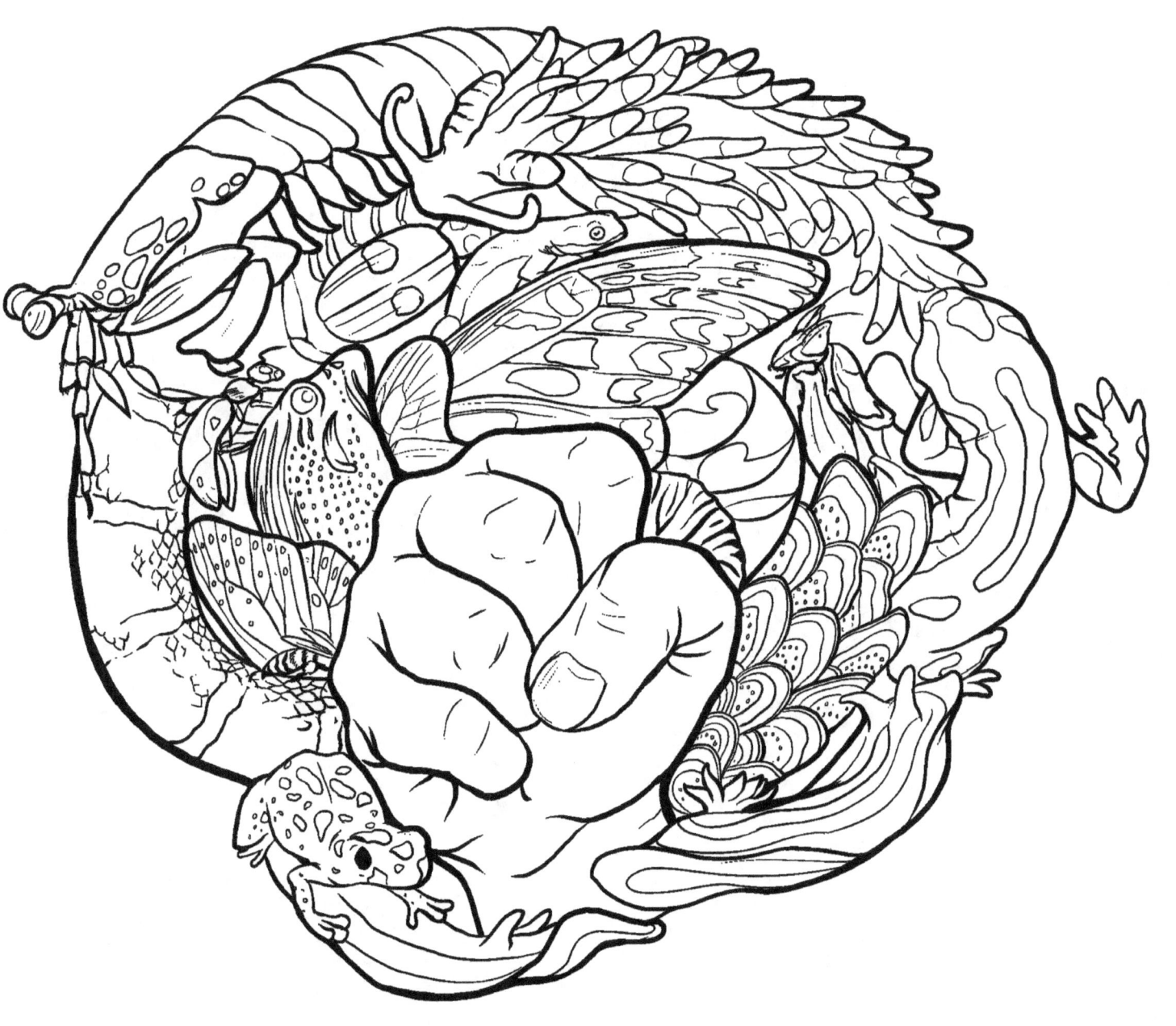

Warn

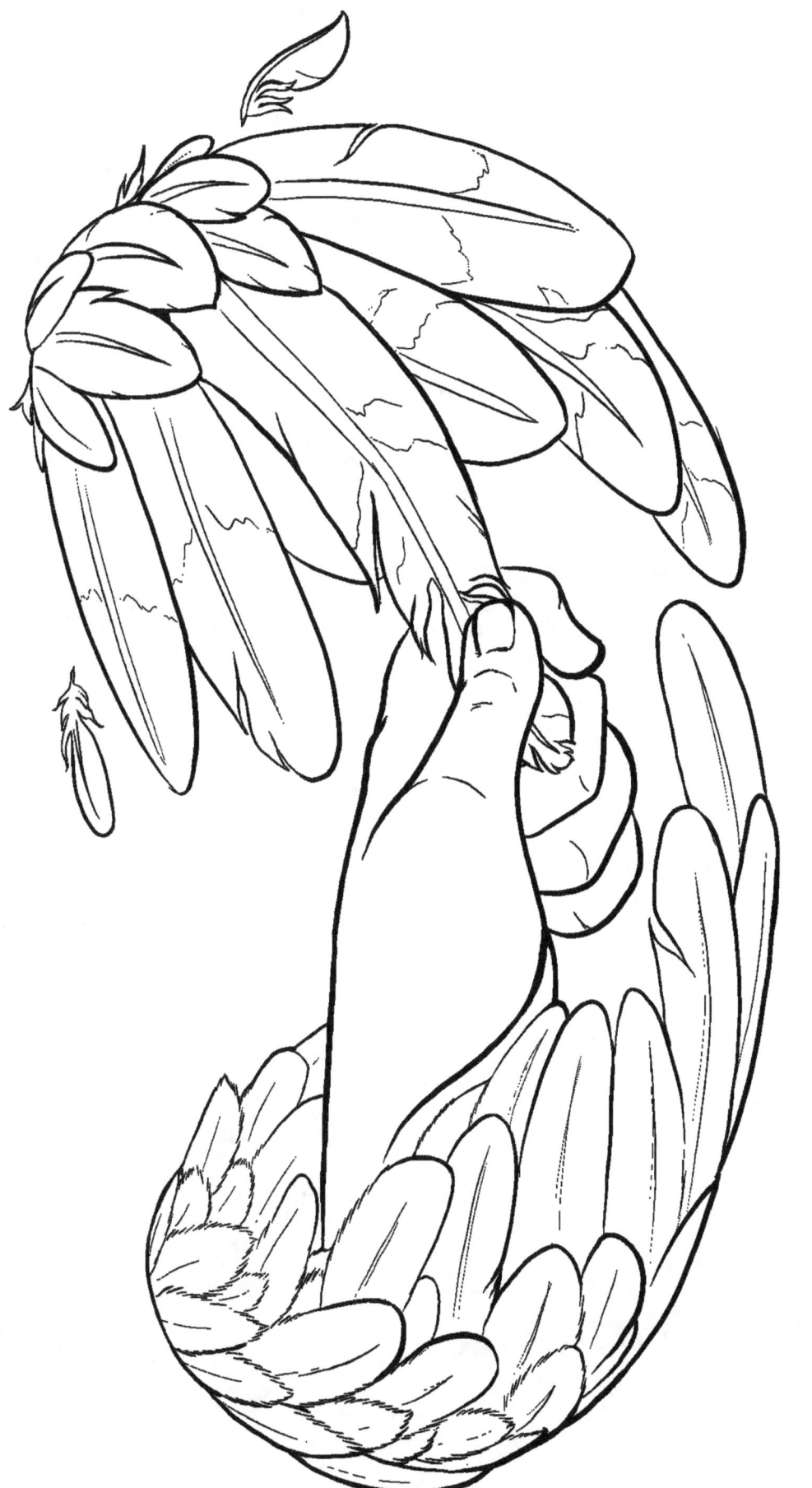

Laugh

Flamboyancy Activities

1. Find a bright, beautiful, wearable object. Draw or write something inspired by it below:

2. Make a plan to wear the object you found. Where will you wear it? Do you want it to be visible to others?

Attract

This drawing is about attracting things towards you. Write or draw things you have to offer in the feathers below, then color it with your favorite colors.

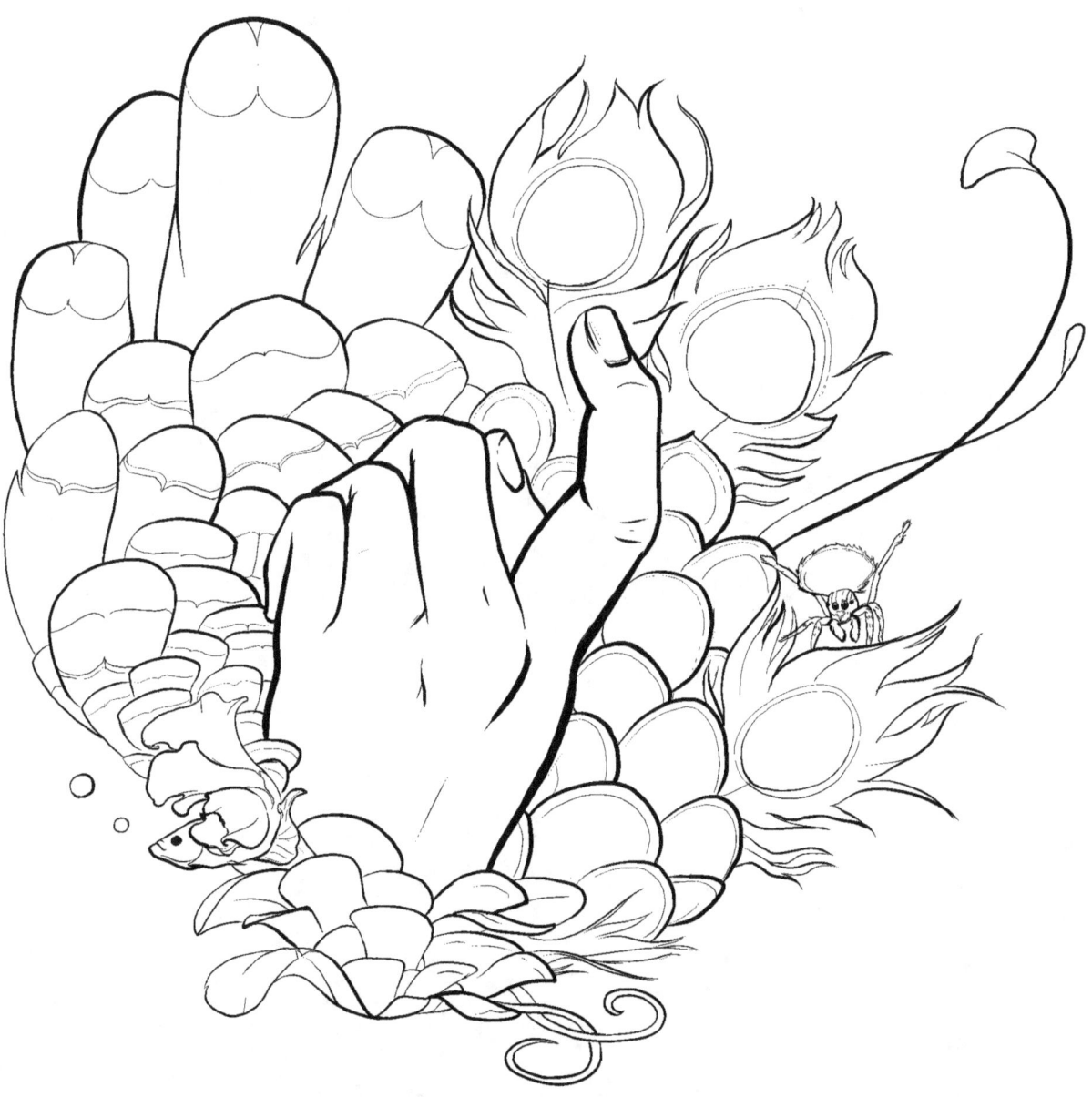

Warn

Fill the empty spaces below with bright patterns and words representing ways you have of defending yourself.

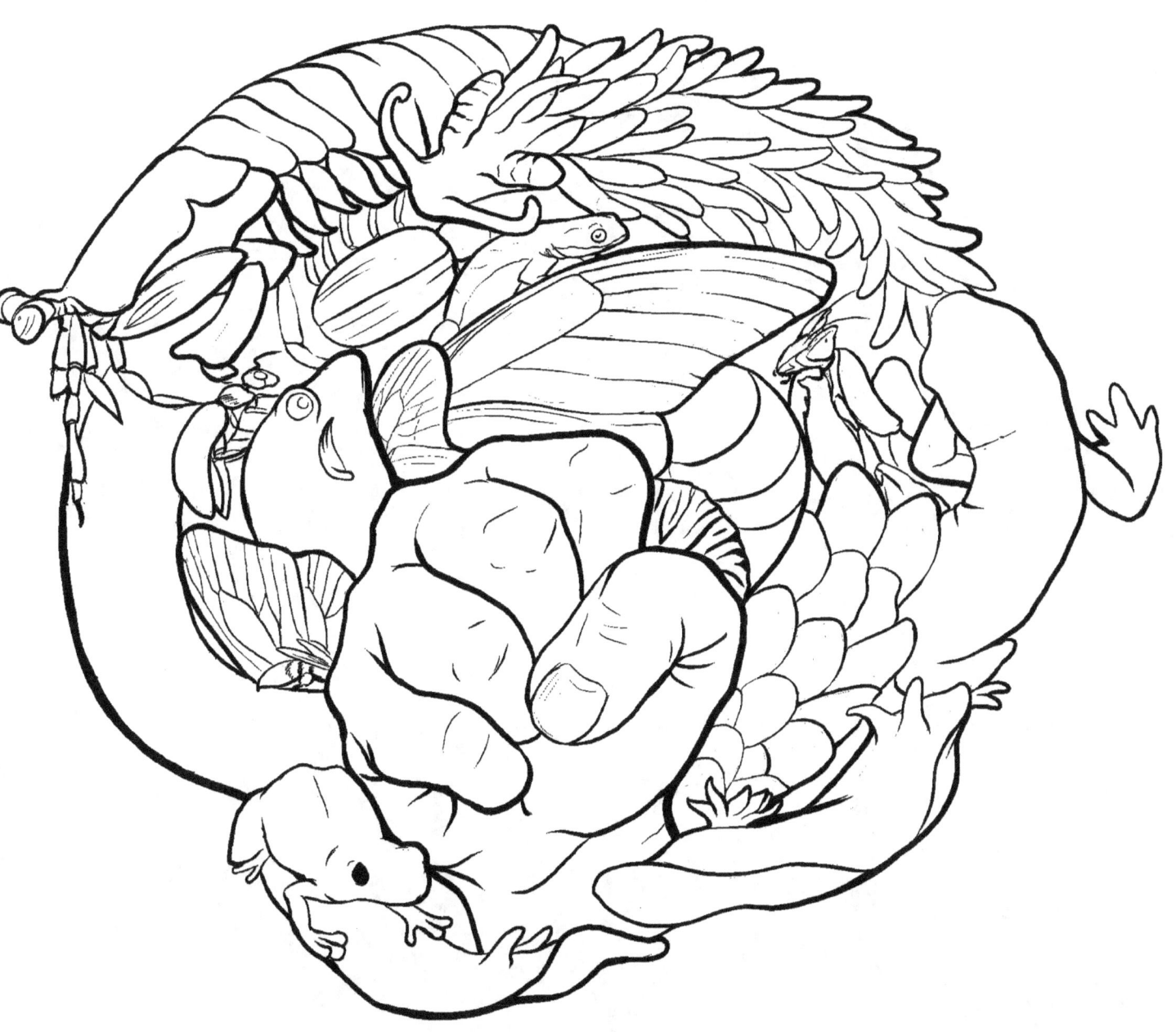

Laugh

Solve the word jumbles below:

GELAE
Hint: symbol of a nation

_____

WRCO
Hint: one of the smartest birds

_____

DOVCIRS
Hint: birds known for trickery

_____

OERPW
Hint: something you have

_____

EUHRLGAT
Hint: makes life lighter

_____

SRTTCEKRI
Hint: one who uses cunning over force

_____

EINEDERCCIS
Hint: colors that aren't what they seem

_____

PERIUSRS
Hint: the unexpected

_____

PSTUE
Hint: a turnabout, reversal of power

_____

RFOEMDE
Hint: a lack of restrictions or coercion

_____

Love

How do you support the ones you care about?

Deeply cooperative relationships can be found throughout nature. Often these cooperative relationships are based in respecting another's needs. Many species of plants have kin recognition, meaning they can tell when the individual plants near them are their siblings, parents, or children. When planted near their kin, they will grow their roots and leaves in a more restrained pattern, growing more straight up and down rather than to the sides. This allows their family members to have better access to sunlight and other resources. Plants can also communicate with each other through the release of various hormones.

Bluegill sunfish, a species common in the Great Lakes, have four genders ("gender" here is defined as a unique set of behaviors and appearances.) Specifically, they have three types of males. The most well-known are larger orange males that will build and fiercely defend a nest site. When a female visits the nest, she leaves her eggs with him and he watches over them throughout the season. The orange males are very territorial of their nests, and some are so aggressive they will attack visiting females as well as rival males and predators. The second type of male is smaller and prefers to sneak into other male's nests, mate with their visiting female, and leave before the larger male can stop them. The third type of male actively courts the orange nest-building male. If his advances are accepted, they will form a partnership and help each other look after the nest and mate with visiting females together for the entire season. It is hypothesized that this male's presence at a nest site helps reassure females that the resident orange male is not overly aggressive and is safe to approach.

Insects are also known to work cooperatively with each other. Honeybees are famous collaborators, sharing duties around the colony and communicating important information to each other. When choosing a new nest site, bees decide democratically, waiting for an 80% consensus before moving forward. Monarch butterflies also cooperate; they are migratory and hibernate in the winter. When the cold begins to set in, hundreds of individual butterflies will cluster together for warmth and safety, an offering of mutual support.

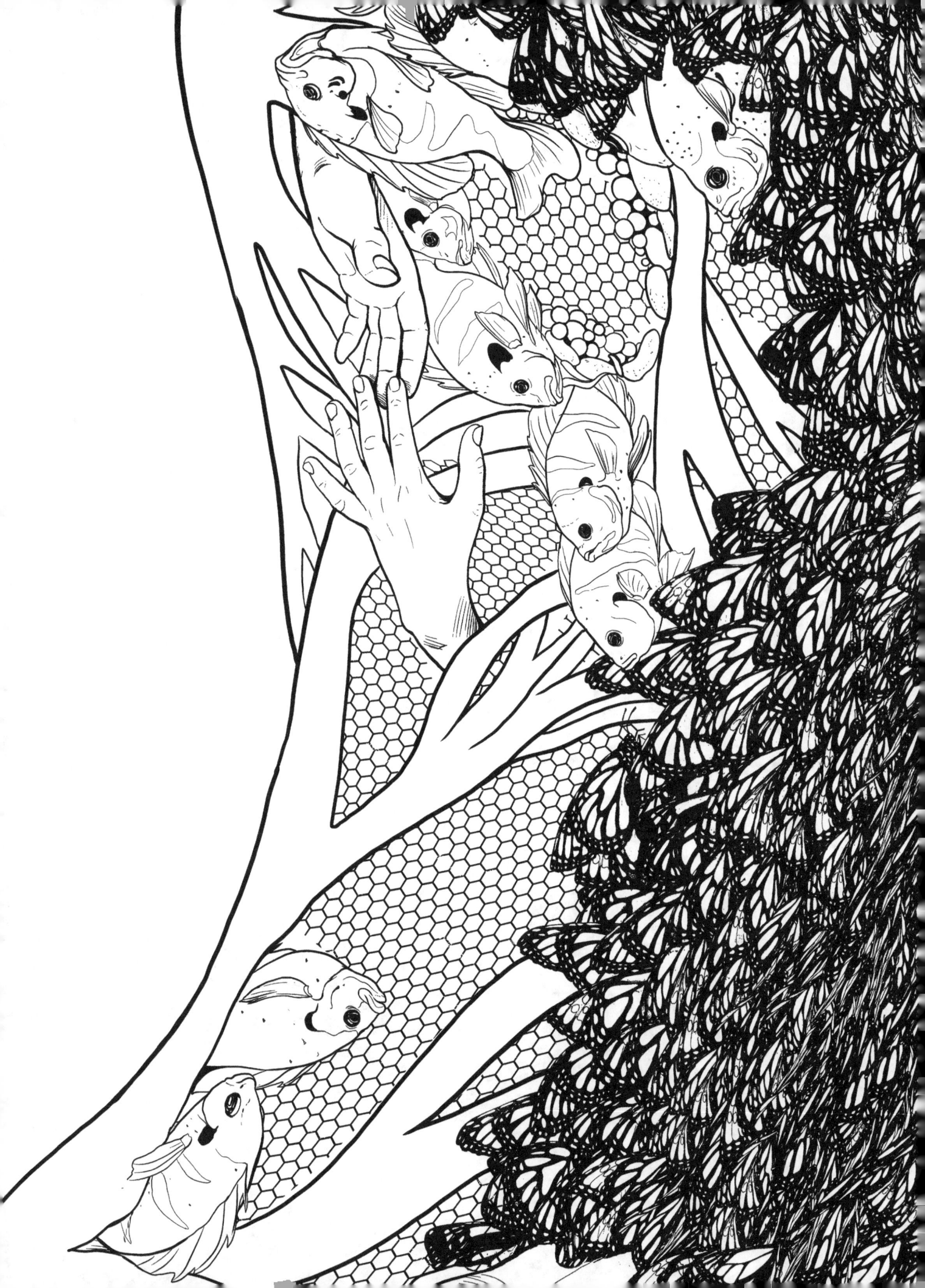

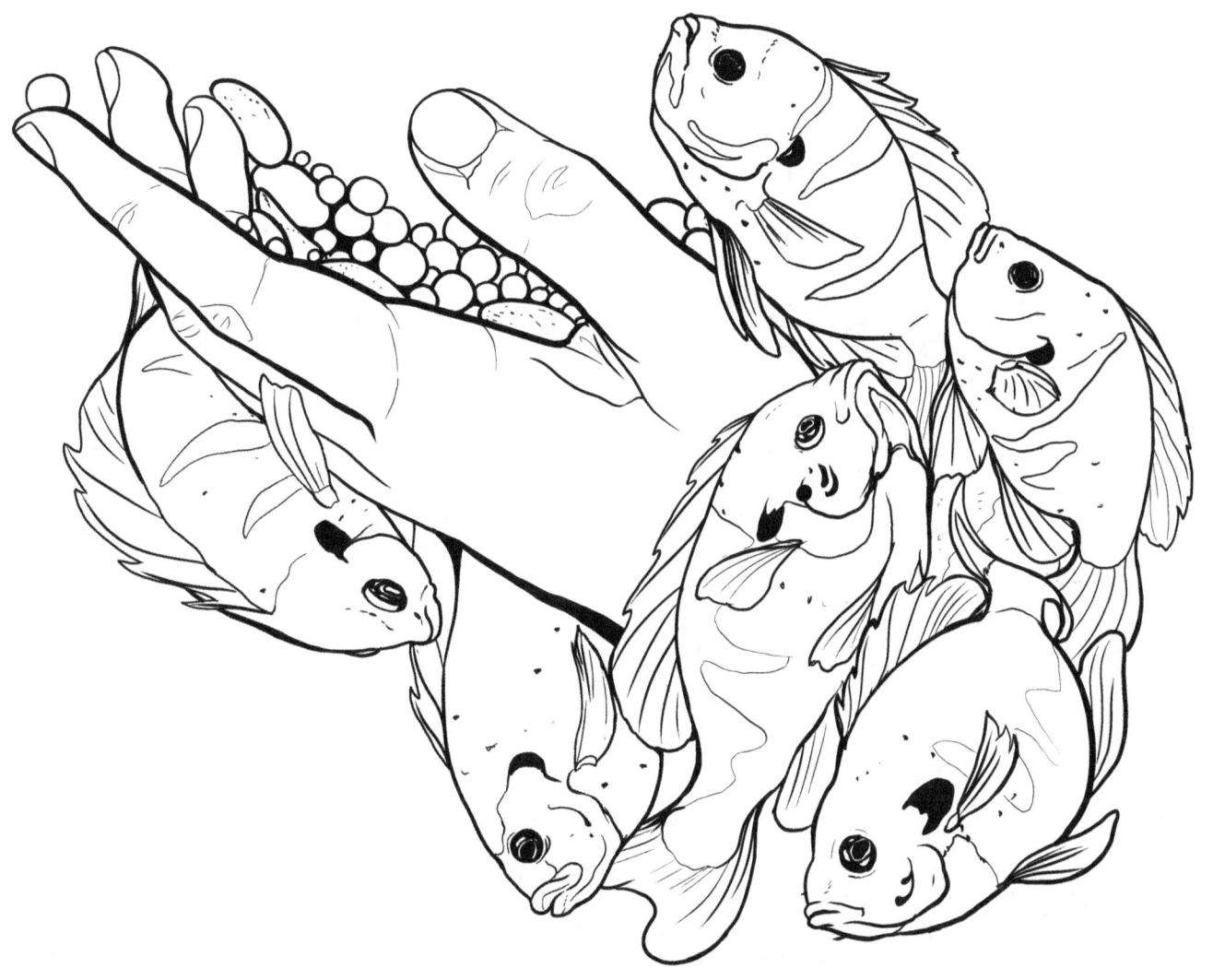

Compassion

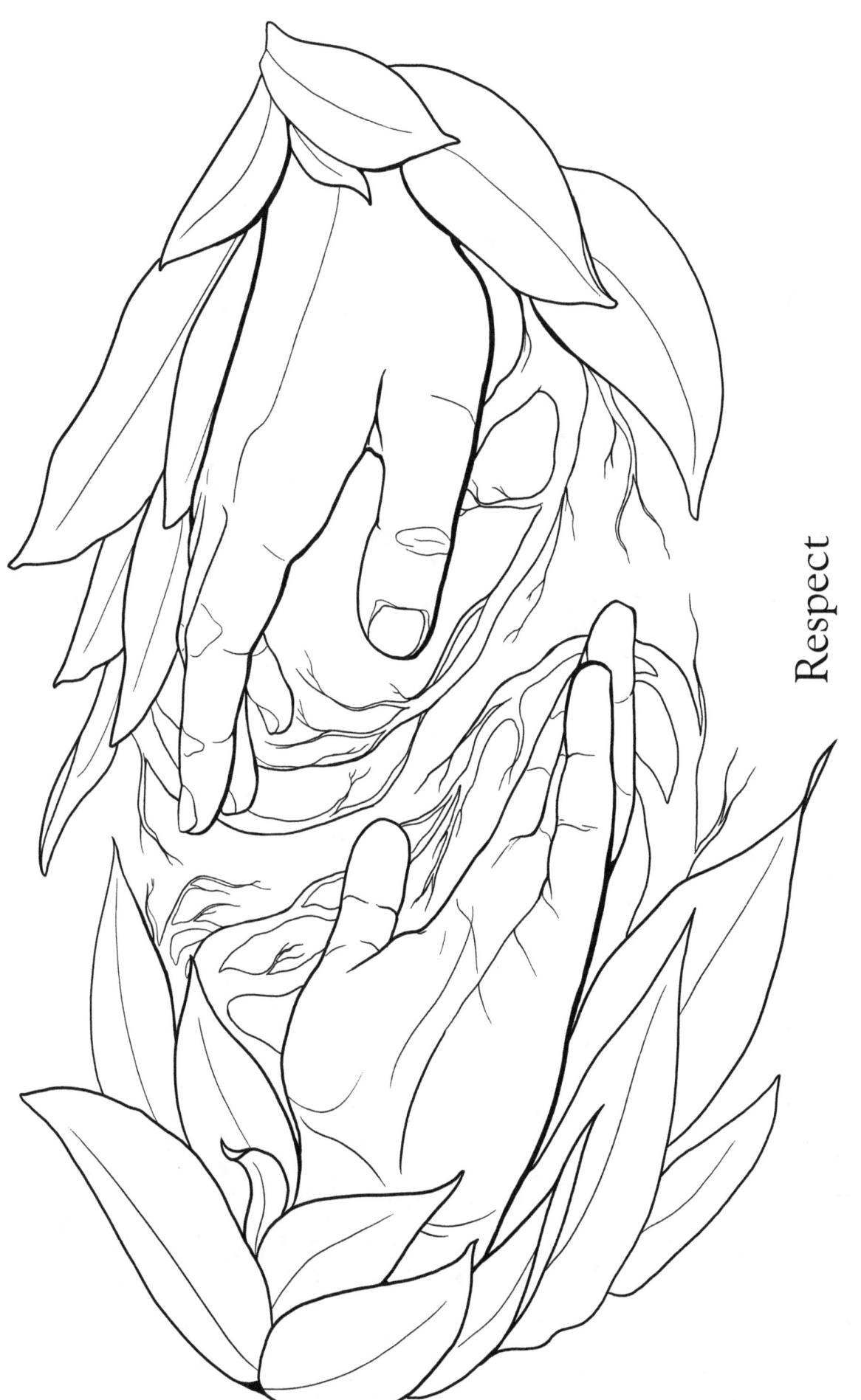

Respect

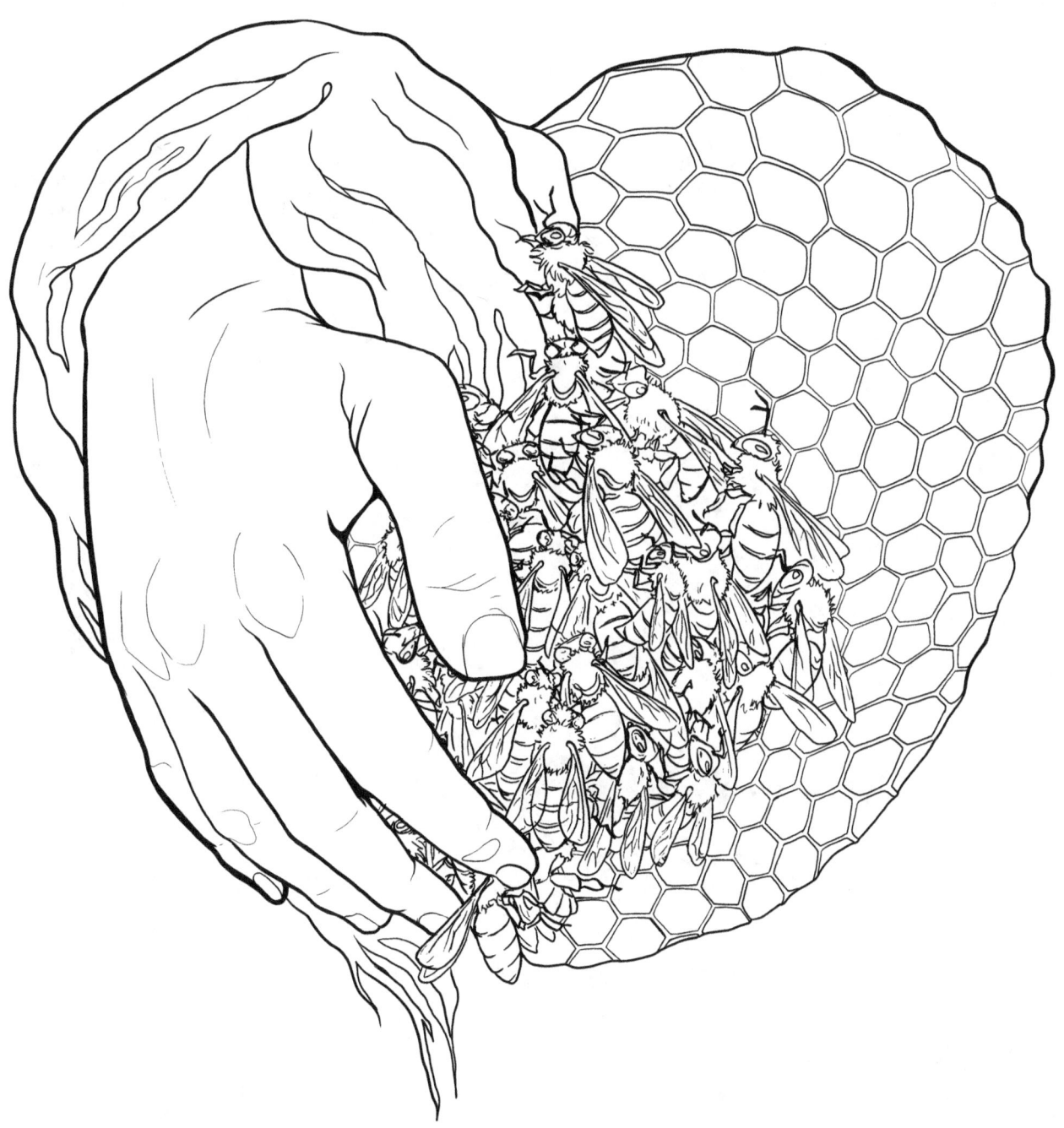

Collaborate

Love Activities

1. Host an event with three or more people. Feed them, talk with them, share space with them, do whatever will be comfortable and nourishing to everyone. Ask them what their favorite flowers are and why, then draw or write about those flowers here:

2. Where can you go to get the most solitude today? What does solitude feel like? Make a few notes or a drawing below.

Compassion

Think of the differences and unique value each person brings to your life. Fill the hand with words or drawings that represent what you create through those compassionate and accepting relationships.

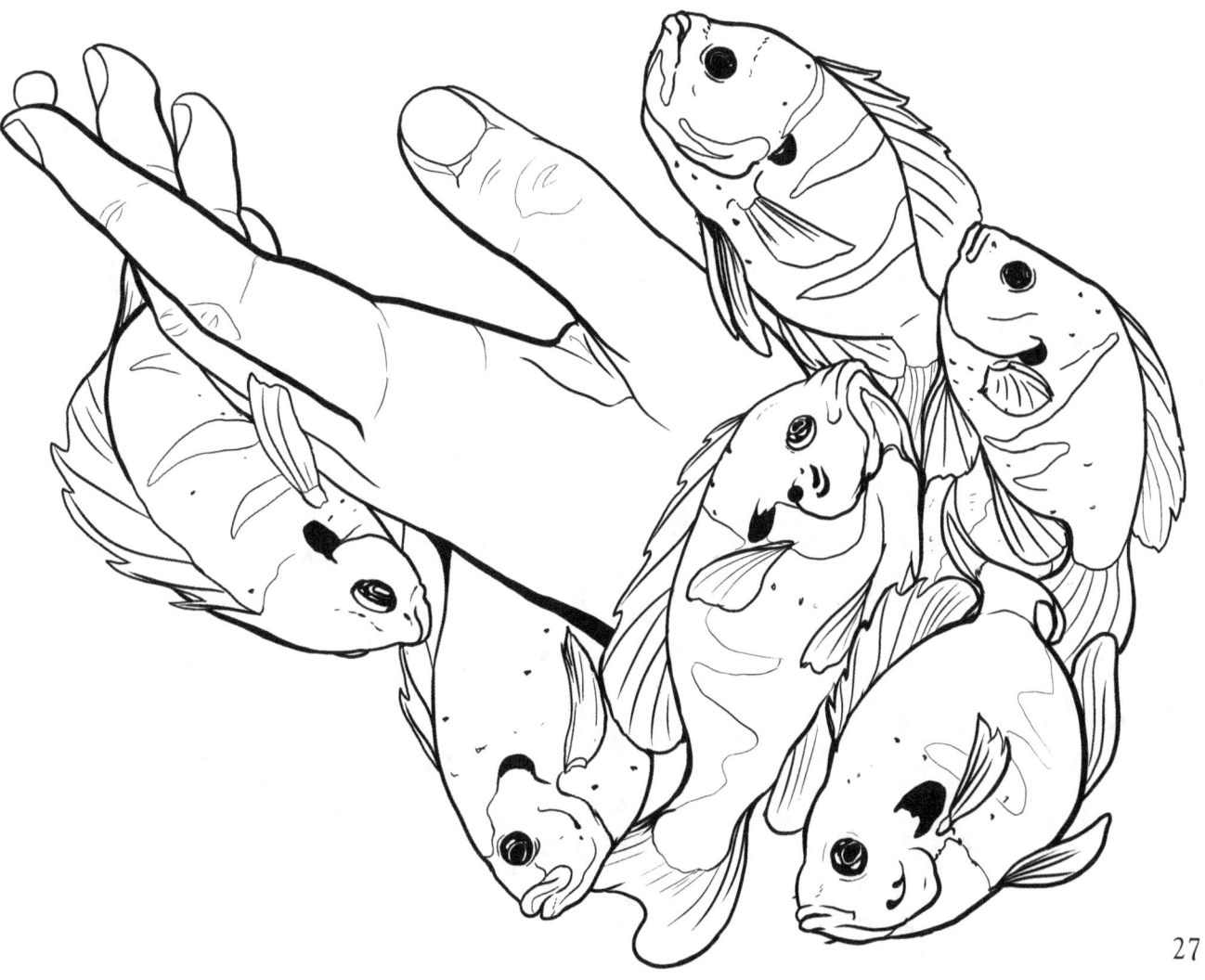

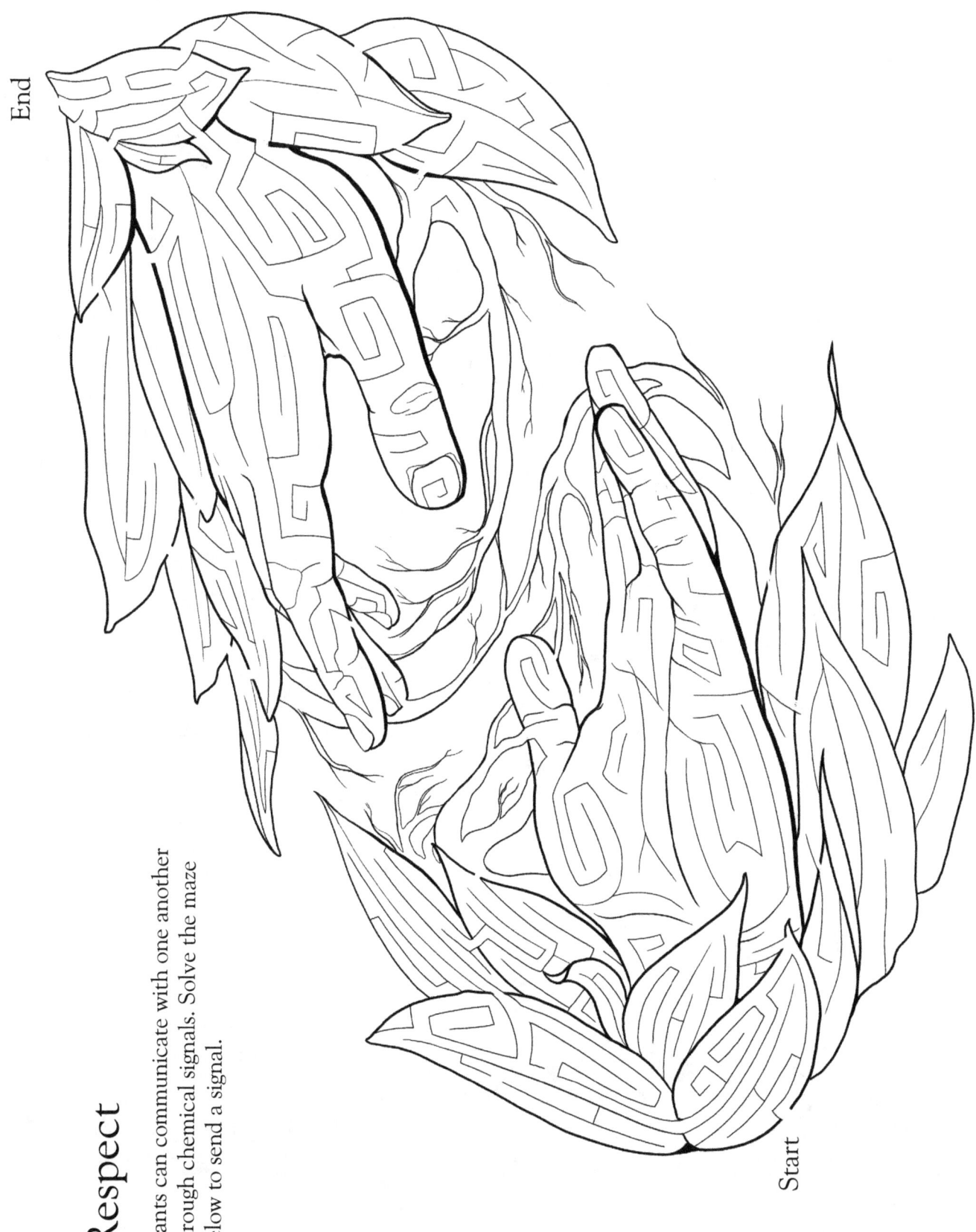

Respect

Plants can communicate with one another through chemical signals. Solve the maze below to send a signal.

End

Start

Collaboration

Start a drawing in the space below, then let a friend finish it.

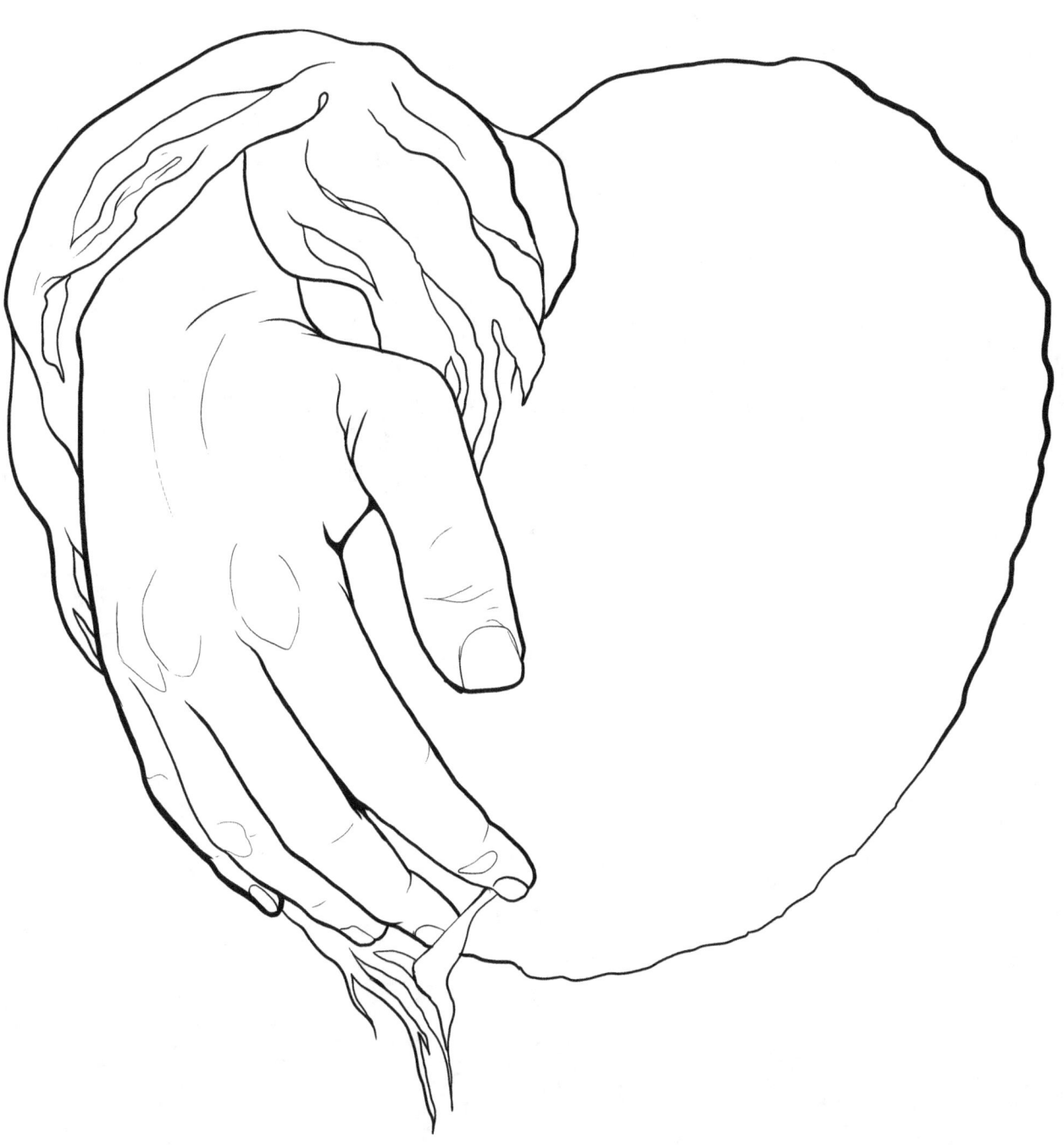

Insight

How do you know and understand the world?

Animals each have their own way of exploring the world and solving problems. Elephants can solve complex problems and use tools. Octopi are notorious escape artists at aquariums, and can solve complicated puzzles such as unscrewing jar lids.

Crows and prairie dogs verbally communicate with one another to share complicated information. Scientists have demonstrated that both animals can not only recognize specific humans, but can also share a description of those humans with others. For example, crows will act aggressively towards certain humans, even if they have never seen or interacted with that human before, if another crow has told them to watch out for a person of that description.

Thismia americana was a species of plant found in Chicago. The plant grew a single small flower and did not photosynthesize. Instead, it got its energy from fungi in rich soil. It is the only species of *Thismia* ever found in the Northern Hemisphere. Specimens of the plant were gathered in the 1910's and then the plant was unseen in the wild for decades. In 2011, a great search was conducted to find any remaining *Thismia americana*.

Hundreds of volunteers searched the remaining prairies near the city and found nothing. Volunteers were also unable to find scale plastic replicas of the flowers that were deliberately planted at certain sites. The area where the flowers were initially found has been paved over, and the species is now believed to be extinct. It's inclusion in this piece is a representation of an ideal goal of insight and cooperation, one that can be elusive at times.

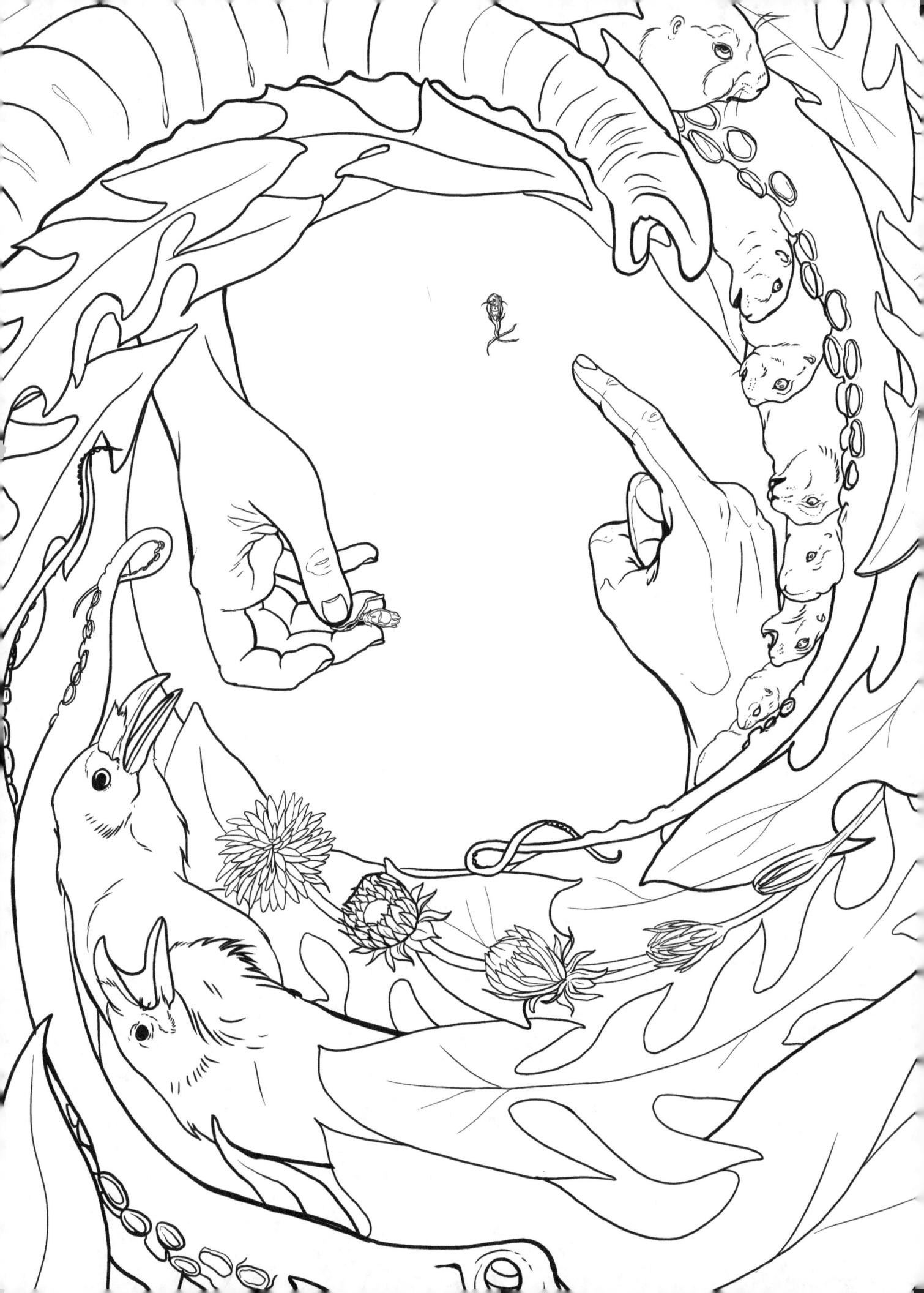

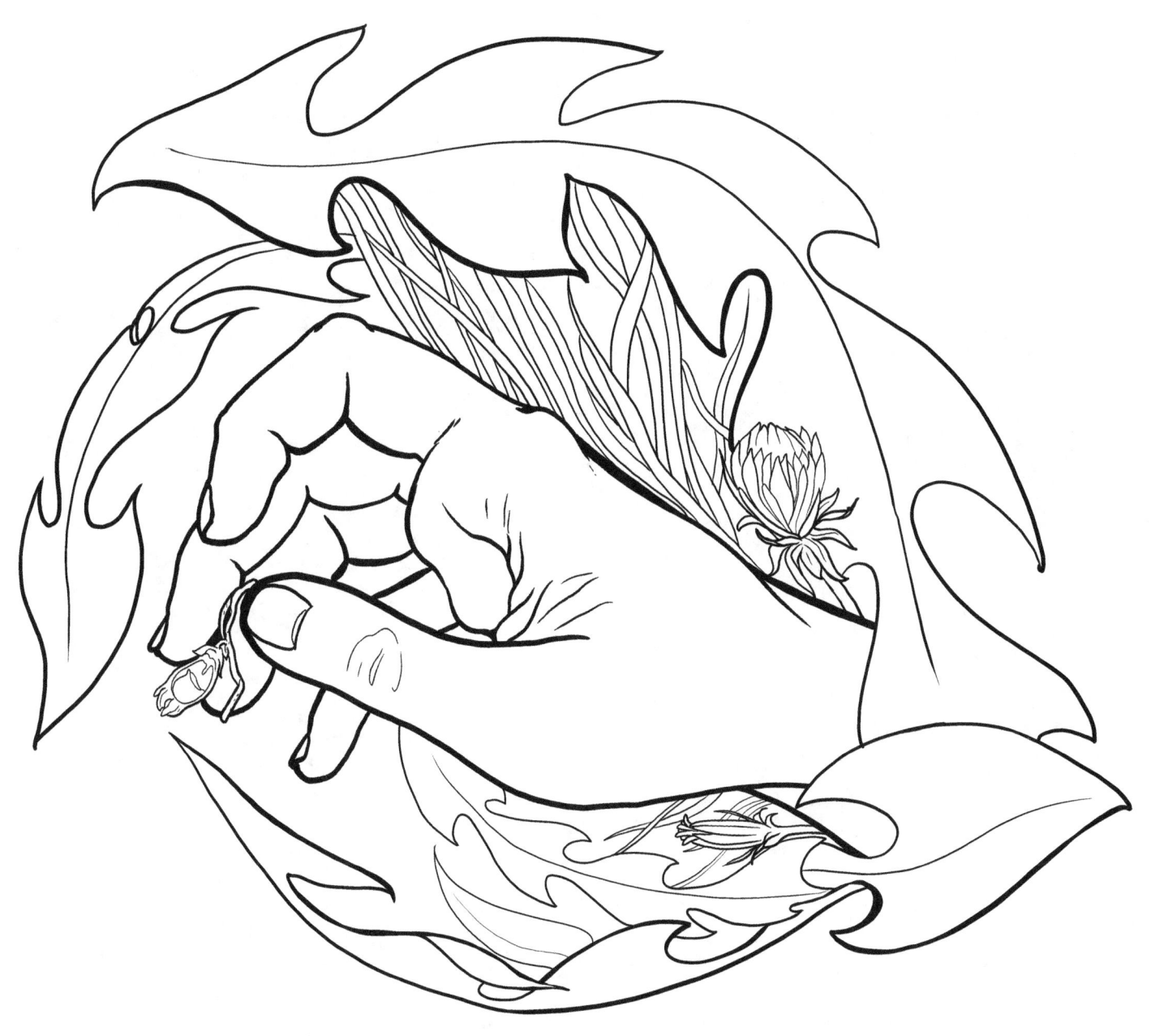

Seek

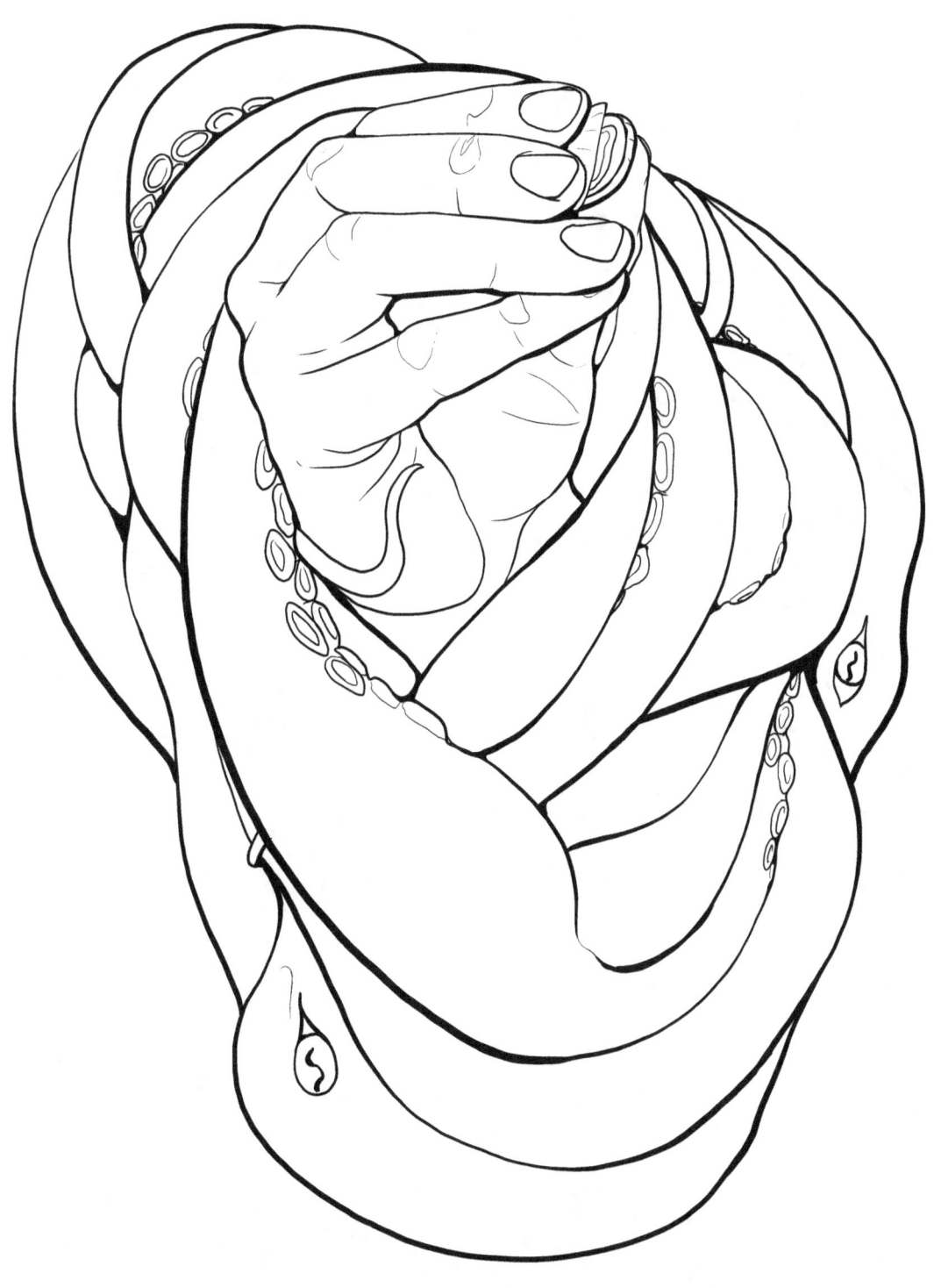

Solve

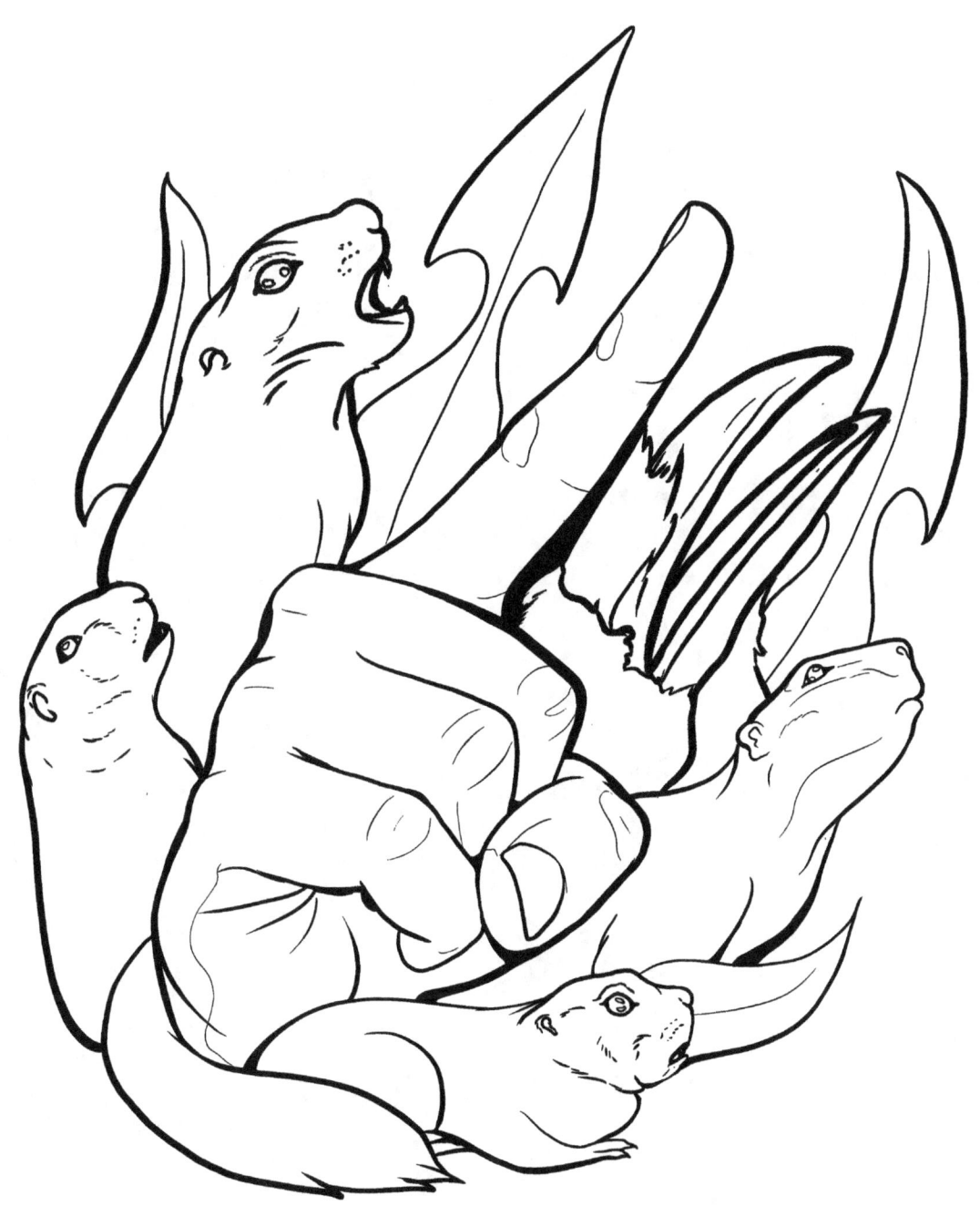

Communicate

Insight Activities

1. Go to a green space, such as your own backyard, a vacant lot, or a park. Find three living creatures there. Try to find something you haven't seen before (look really closely if you have to!) What are they doing? Write down or draw your observations.

2. In a way that's safe for you, try copying some of the animal and plant behaviors you've noticed. Act them out, dance, or try a new approach to a problem you've been trying to solve.

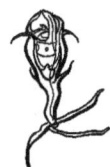

Seek

Find 7 *Thismia americana* in the drawing below.

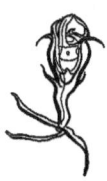

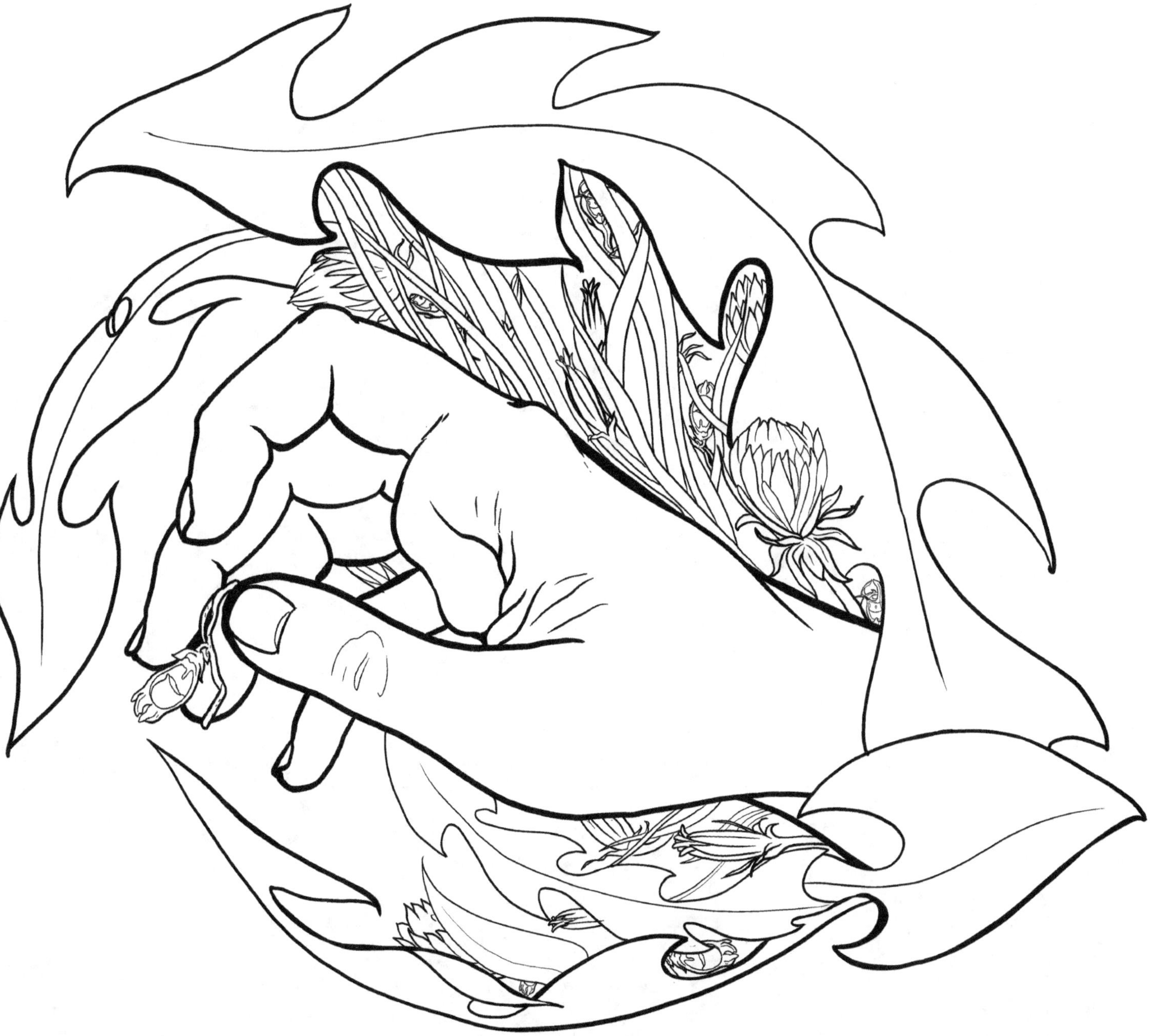

Solve

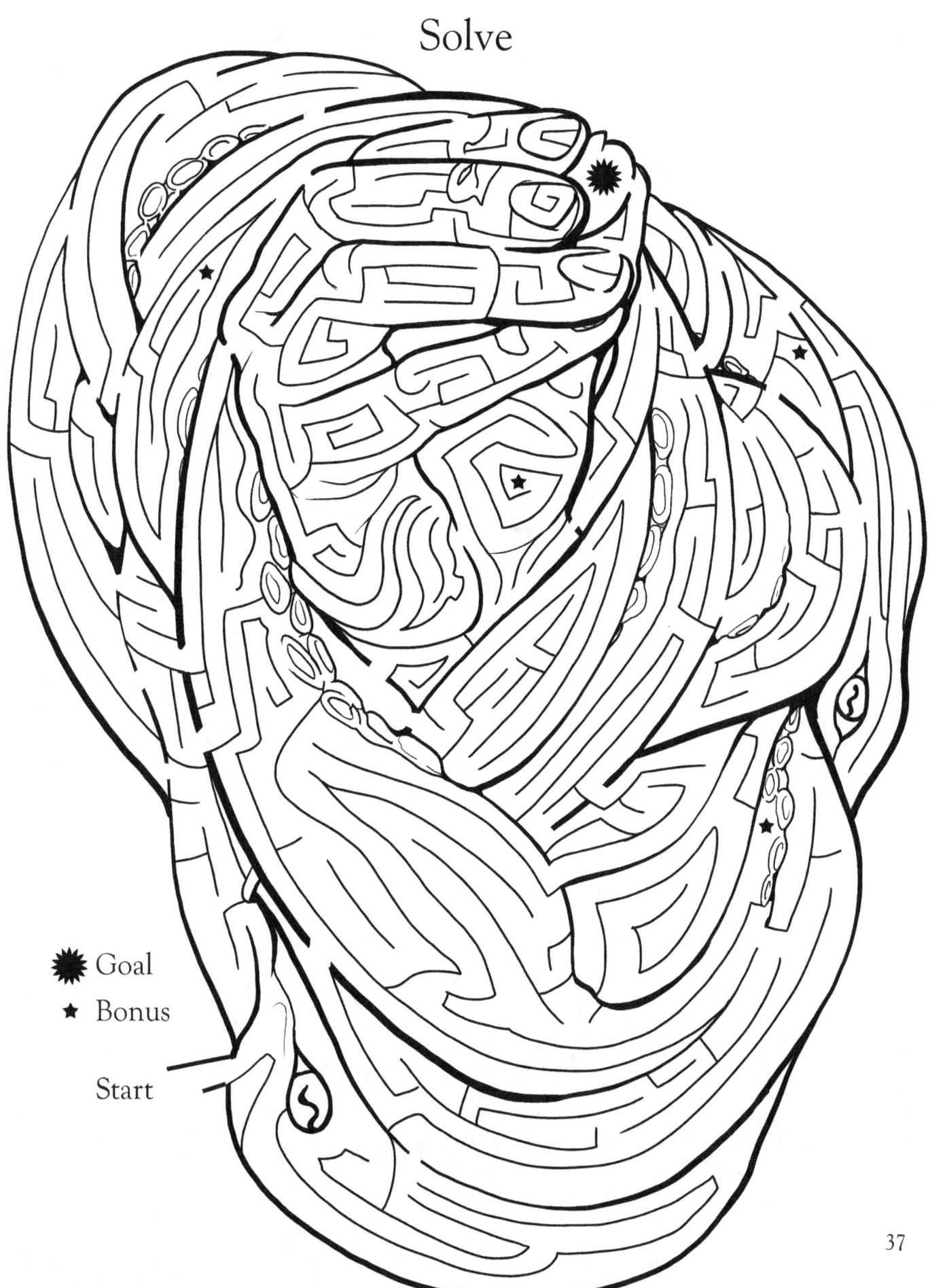

🟊 Goal

★ Bonus

Start

37

Communicate

Solve the word jumbles below:

NSGTINILE
Hint: to hear what others have to say

_____

PTUSPGONIR
Hint: to give assistance and affirmation

_____

EGRLNINA
Hint: to gain knowledge and information

_____

NILBIGUD
Hint: to create a community or space

_____

GSIARNH
Hint: to give information to another

_____

EDGIFNEDN
Hint: to protect and corroborate

_____

NIRAGNW
Hint: information about safety

_____

OGMNITAVIT
Hint: to encourage, inspire, and support

_____

ONLVISG
Hint: to arrive at a solution to a problem

_____

NALTBGIRCEE
Hint: to hold in joy and respect

_____

Passion

What is something you desperately want? Remember that feeling.

Desire, anger, and determination can be equally destructive or constructive forces in our lives. A raw drive for something to be *different* can help us move through tangles of doubt and depression, encourage us to connect with others, or fuel the actions that push back against toxic social ideas.

The plants around the edges of this piece are garlic mustard leaves—an invasive plant species that chokes out native plants and releases antifungal chemicals into the ground that disrupt native plant species' essential relationships with fungi. This pervasiveness and disruption of vital relationships is reminiscent of how bigotry and systematic oppression can function.

Wildfire and prescribed burns clear out dead undergrowth and invasive species, and revitalize the soil for native plants. When lava flows out of the earth, it both creates and destroys. New land is being formed all the time by lava under the ocean.

Many animals provided inspiration for this part of the series. Birds will defend their nests from intruders, and japanese honeybees will swarm over invading hornets, cooking them alive with their own body heat rather than let them threaten the hive.

Garter snakes hibernate in mass nests. When they emerge in the spring, they take mating embraces with both males and females, warming themselves and each other. Antechinus is a genus of marsupials known for having only one short and frantic breeding season during their lifetimes.

Many animals travel vast distances during their migrations. Others find ways to survive in hostile environments like deep sea vents, with boiling water and no sunlight.

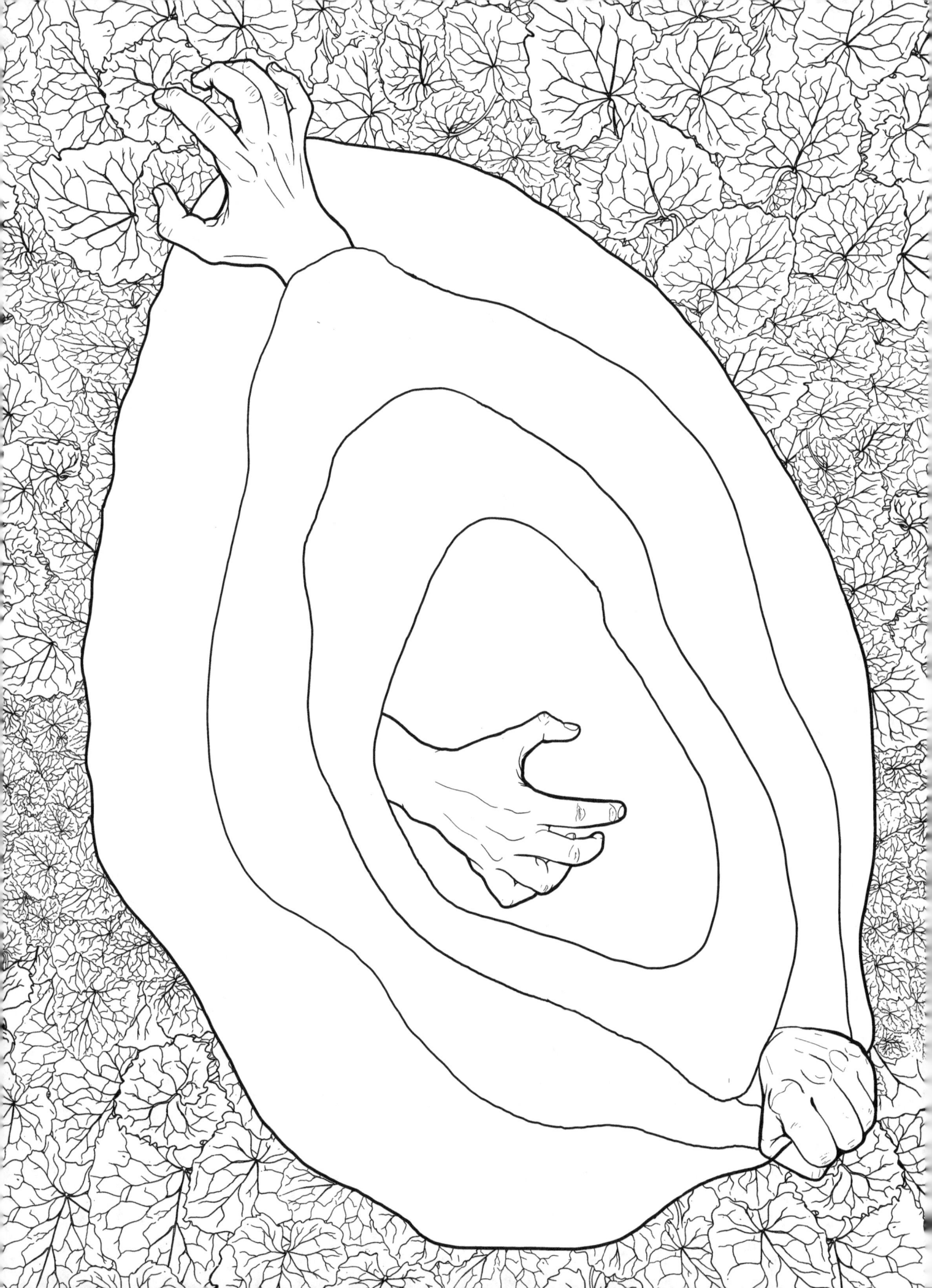

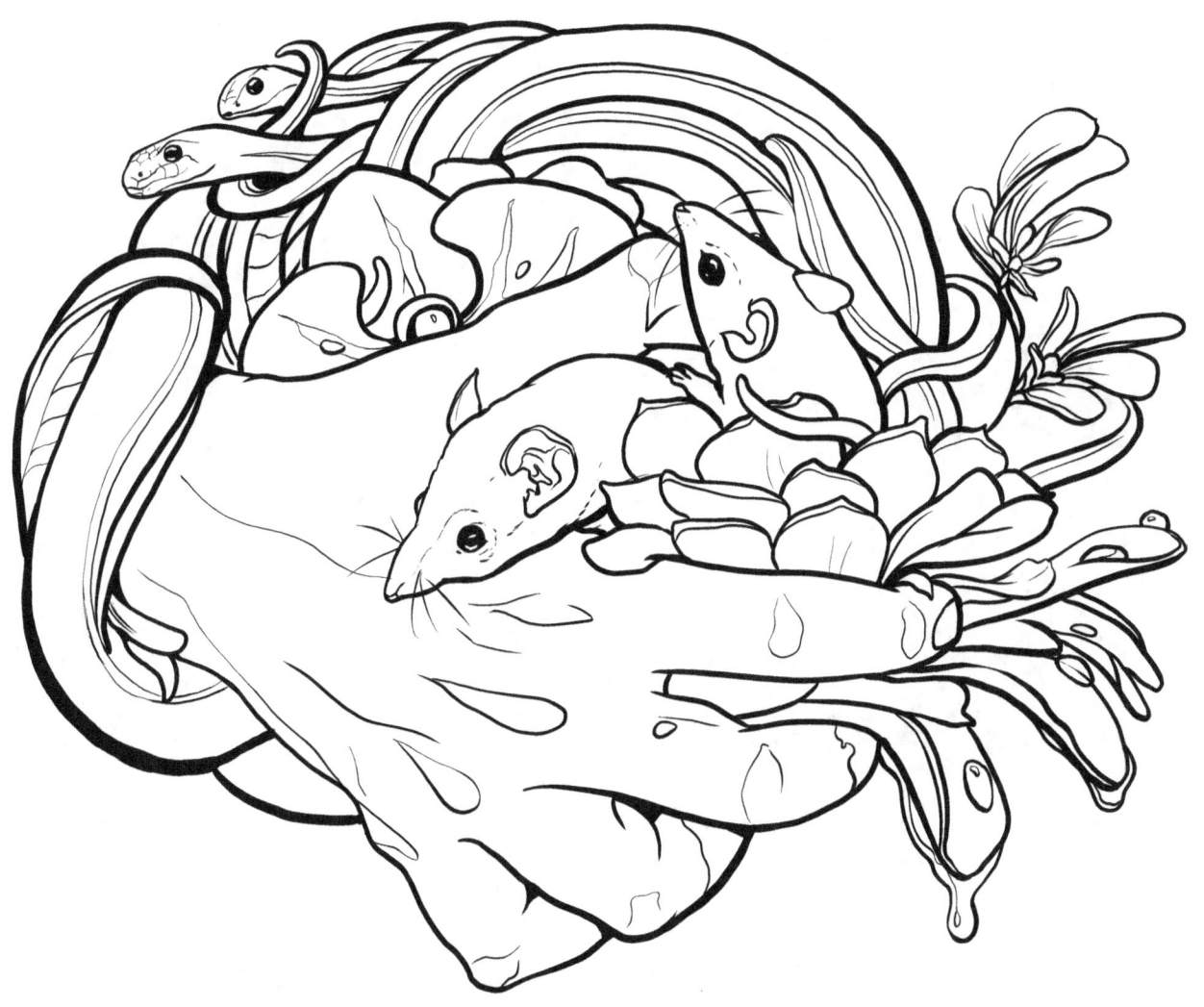

Desire

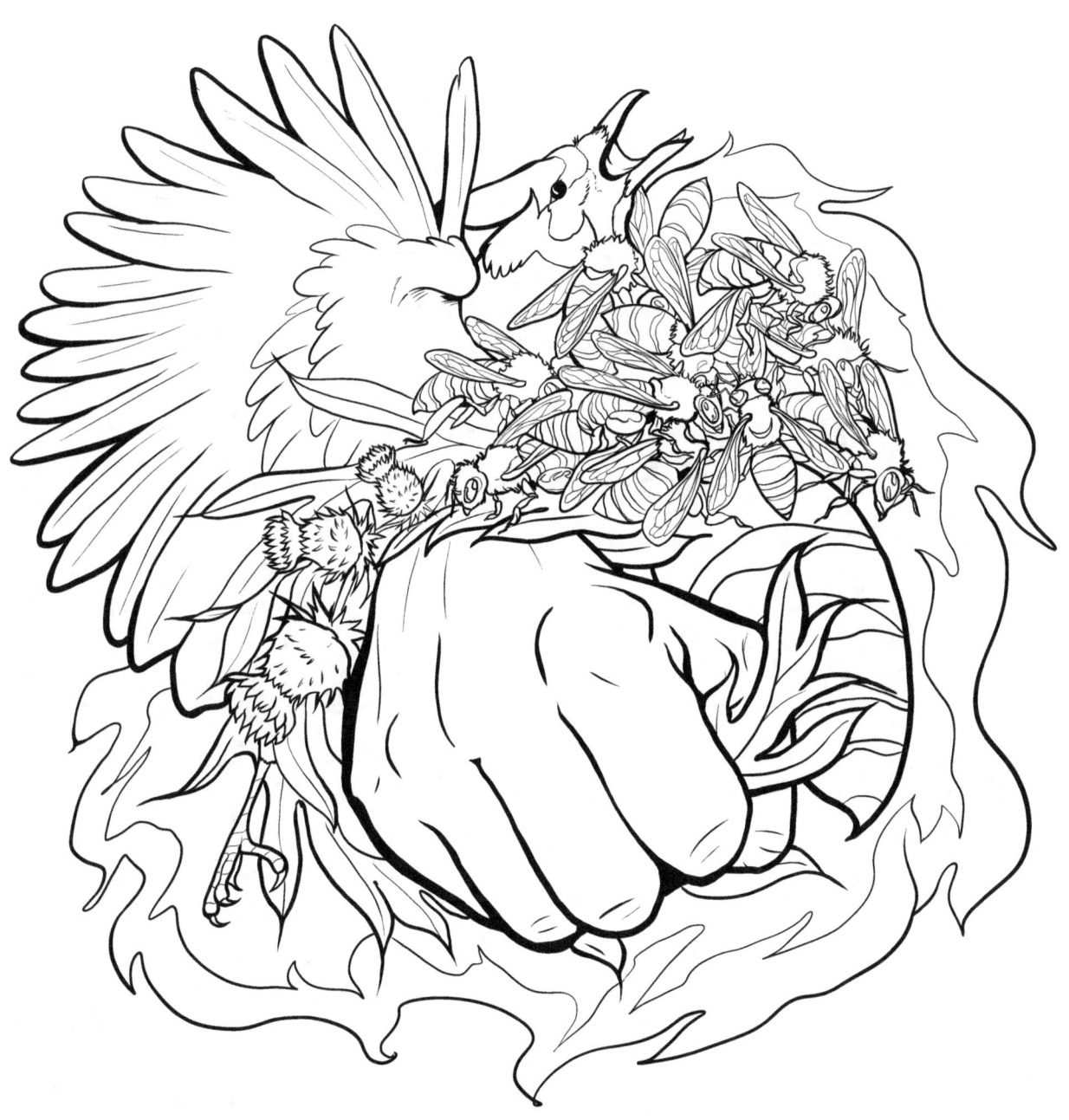

Anger

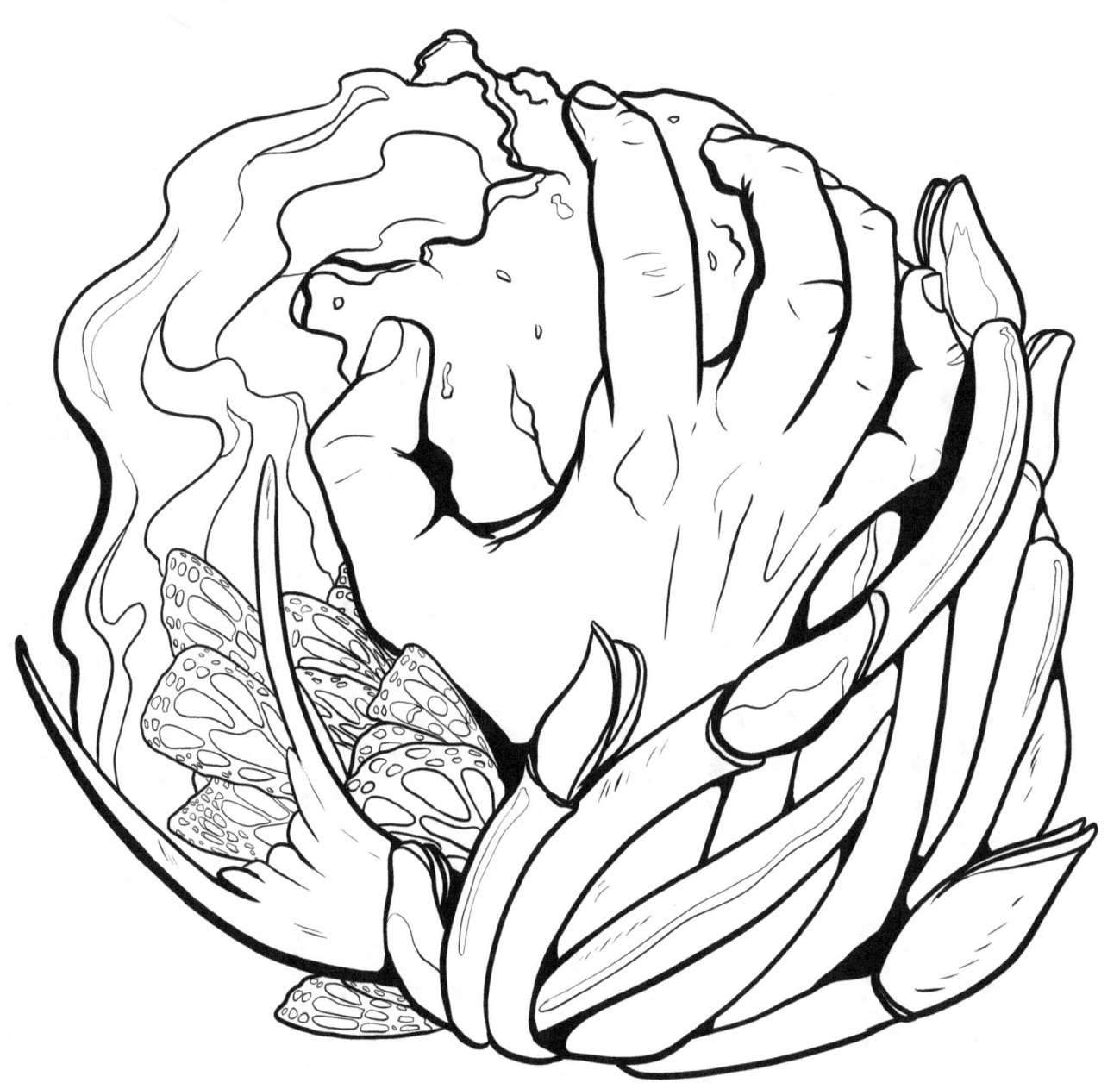

Determination

Passion Activities

1. Make a small change to your environment: tidy up one or two objects, put some new art on the wall, or change the lighting.

2. Think of something you want to have in your community. Try drawing it below, even if it's only stick figures.

Desire

What is something you want? Draw it here.

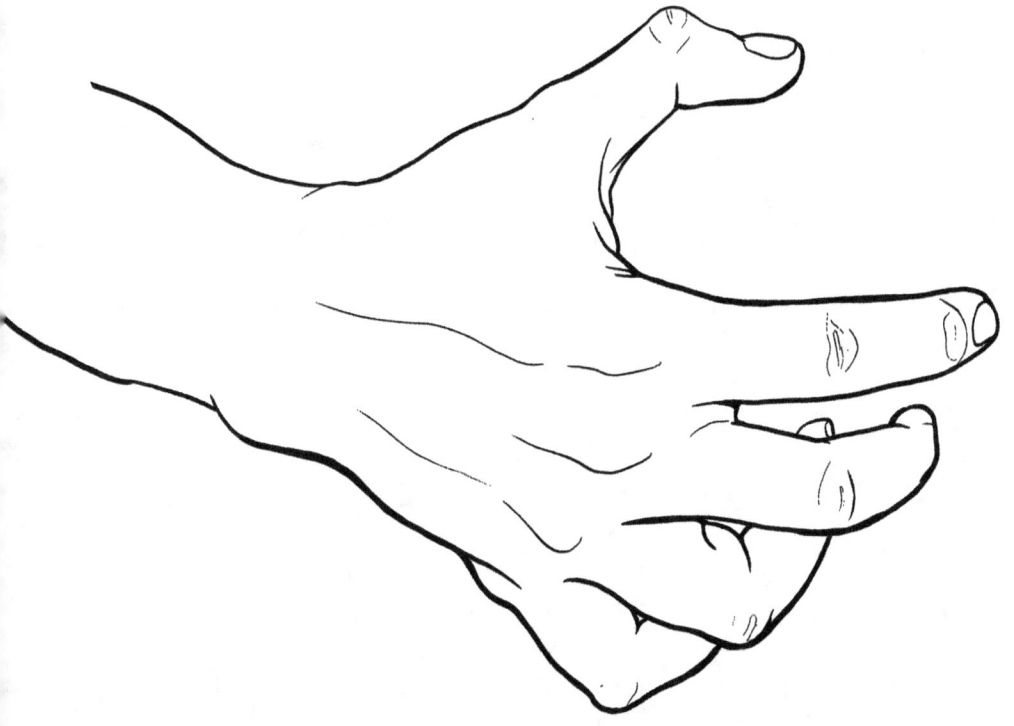

Anger

Anger is most valuable when you understand what's within it. Connect the dots below, then refine the lines and color to bring clarity to anger.

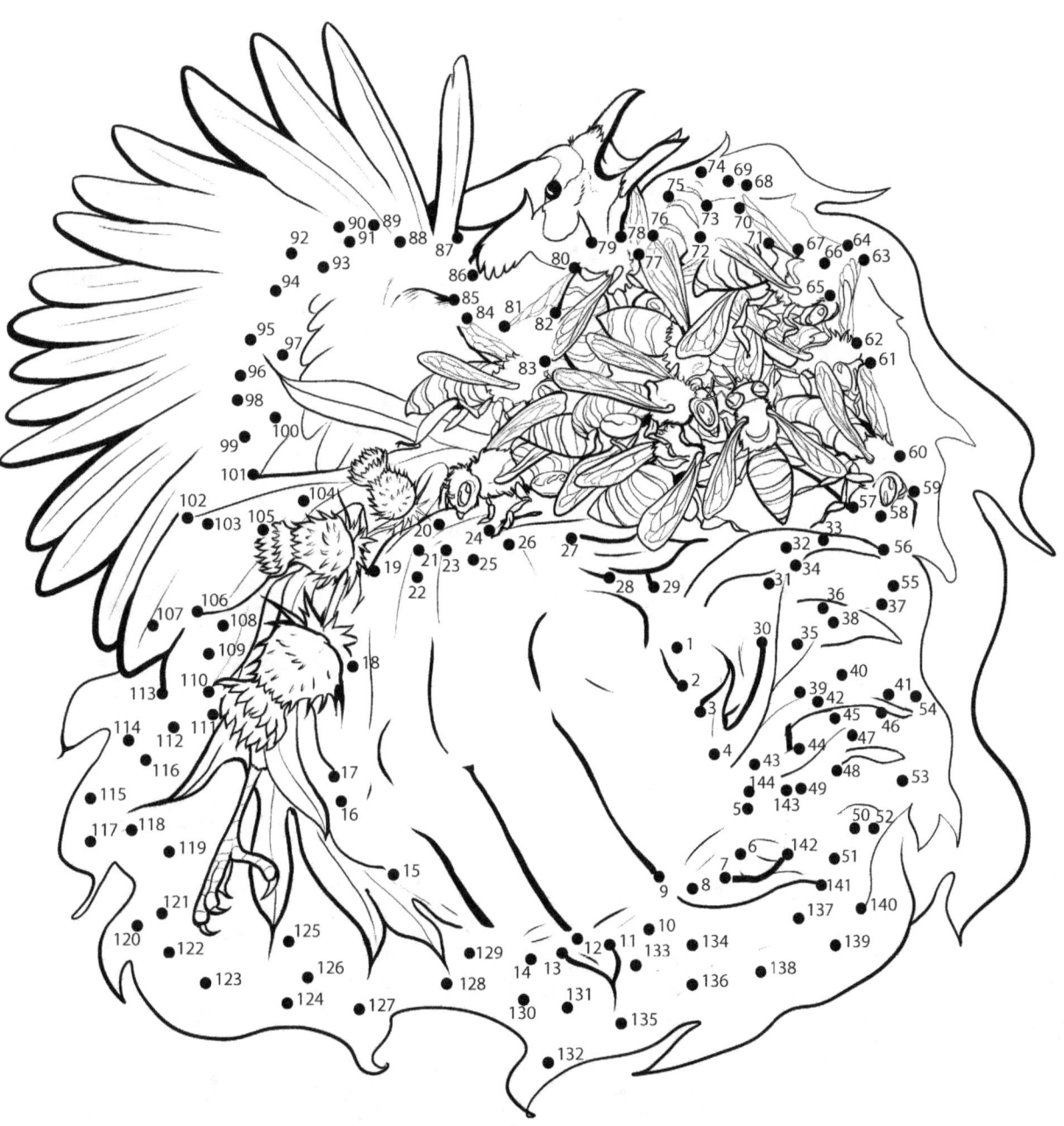

Determination

Determination is a mix of willpower and patience. Fill the spaces below with dark and light cross-hatching.

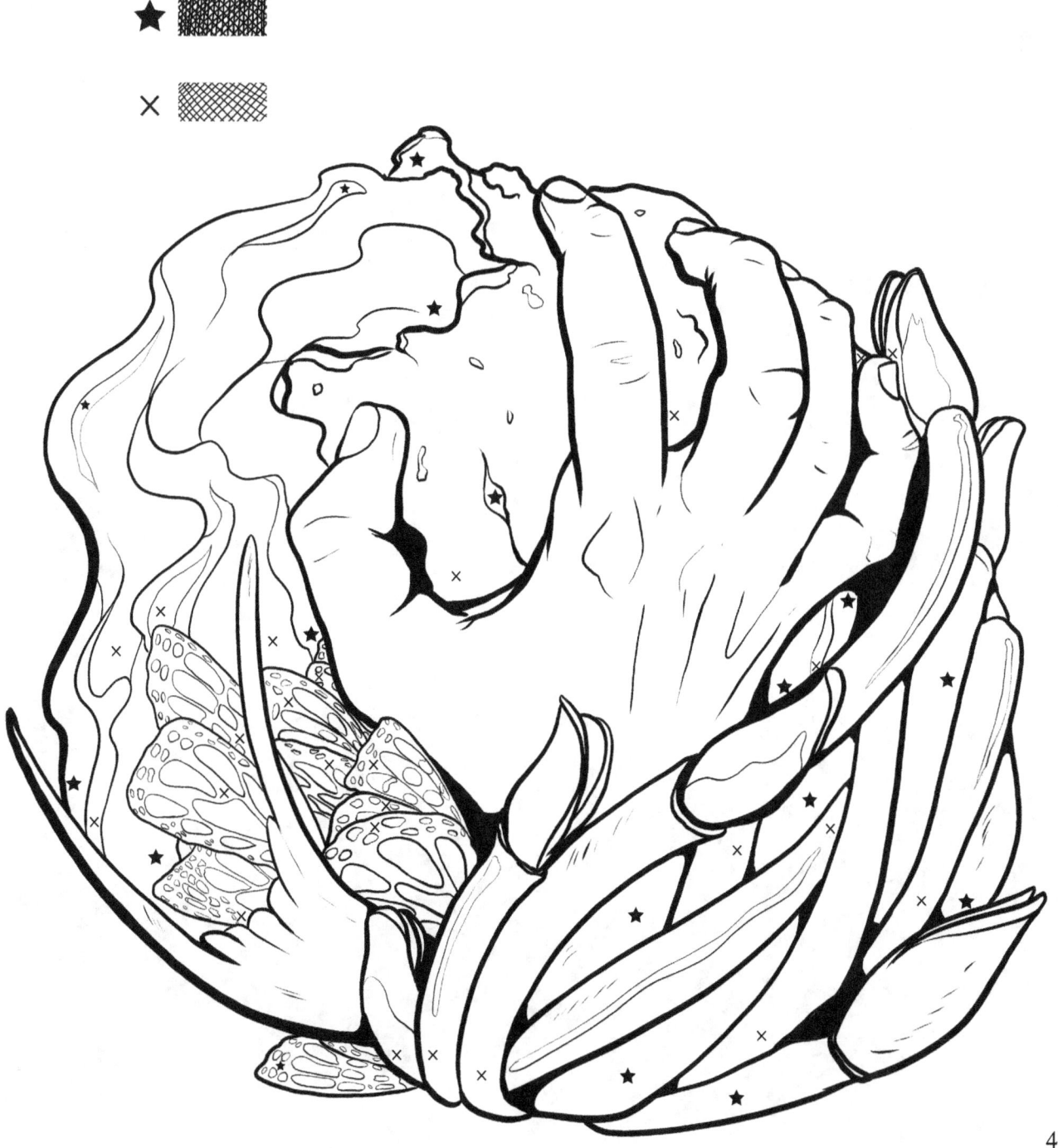

Transformation

How do you enact change? How do you accept change?

Nature is in a constant state of transformation. Leaves unfurl, thrive, and fall. Snakes are often symbols of transformation, shedding old skins in a constant cycle of renewal. Insects like these dragonflies emerge from their eggs as nymphs, flightless for the first year or two of their lives. They eventually remake themselves, emerging from their old skins and unfolding their wings for the first time.

It can be helpful to remember that change happens in stages, and the results of a change may be surprising. Gynandromorph butterflies (like the swallowtails featured here) are genetic mosaics, both male and female, and have a patchwork coloration of both male and female characteristics. These characteristics are not usually apparent until after the caterpillar has emerged as a butterfly.

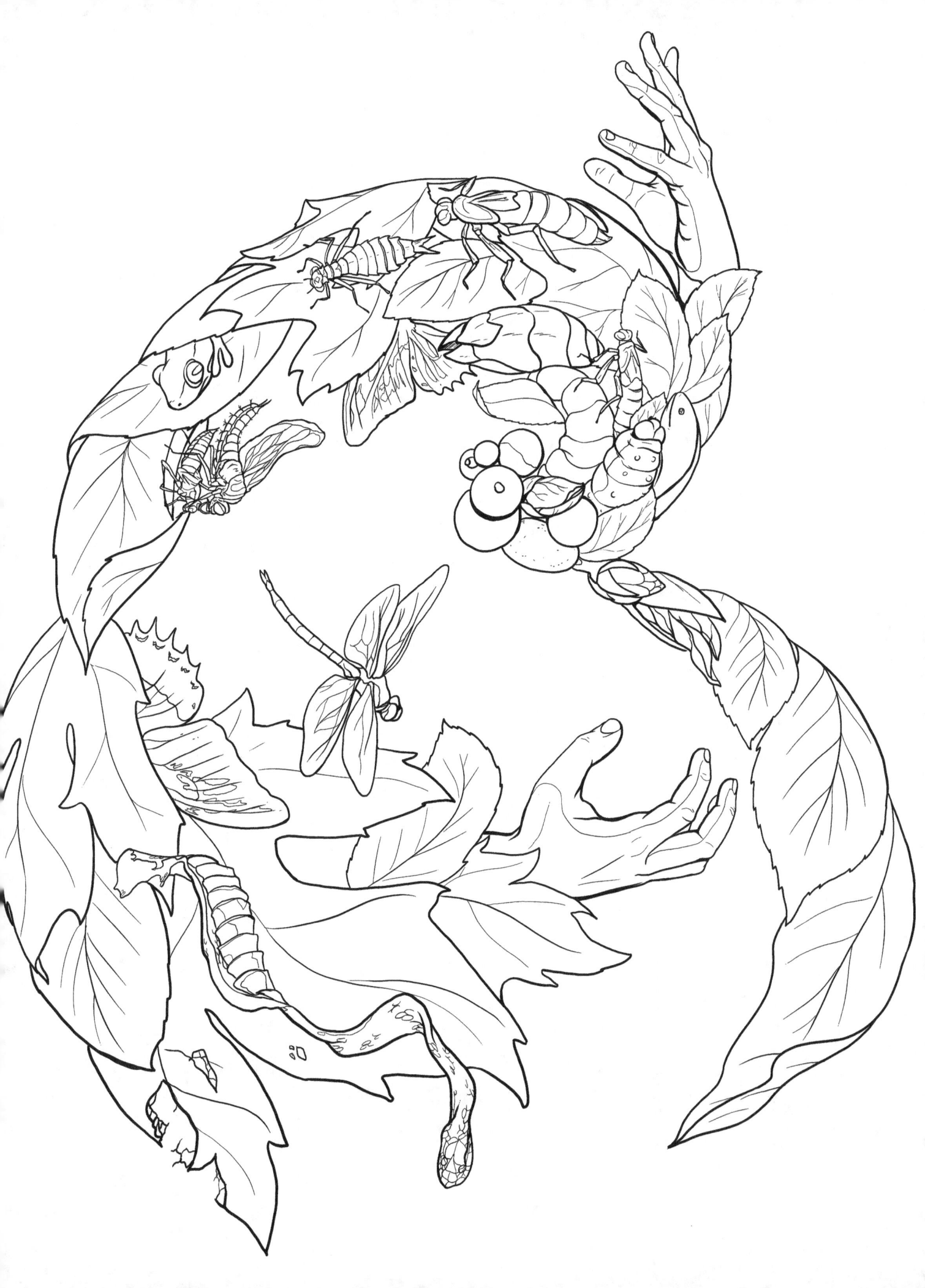

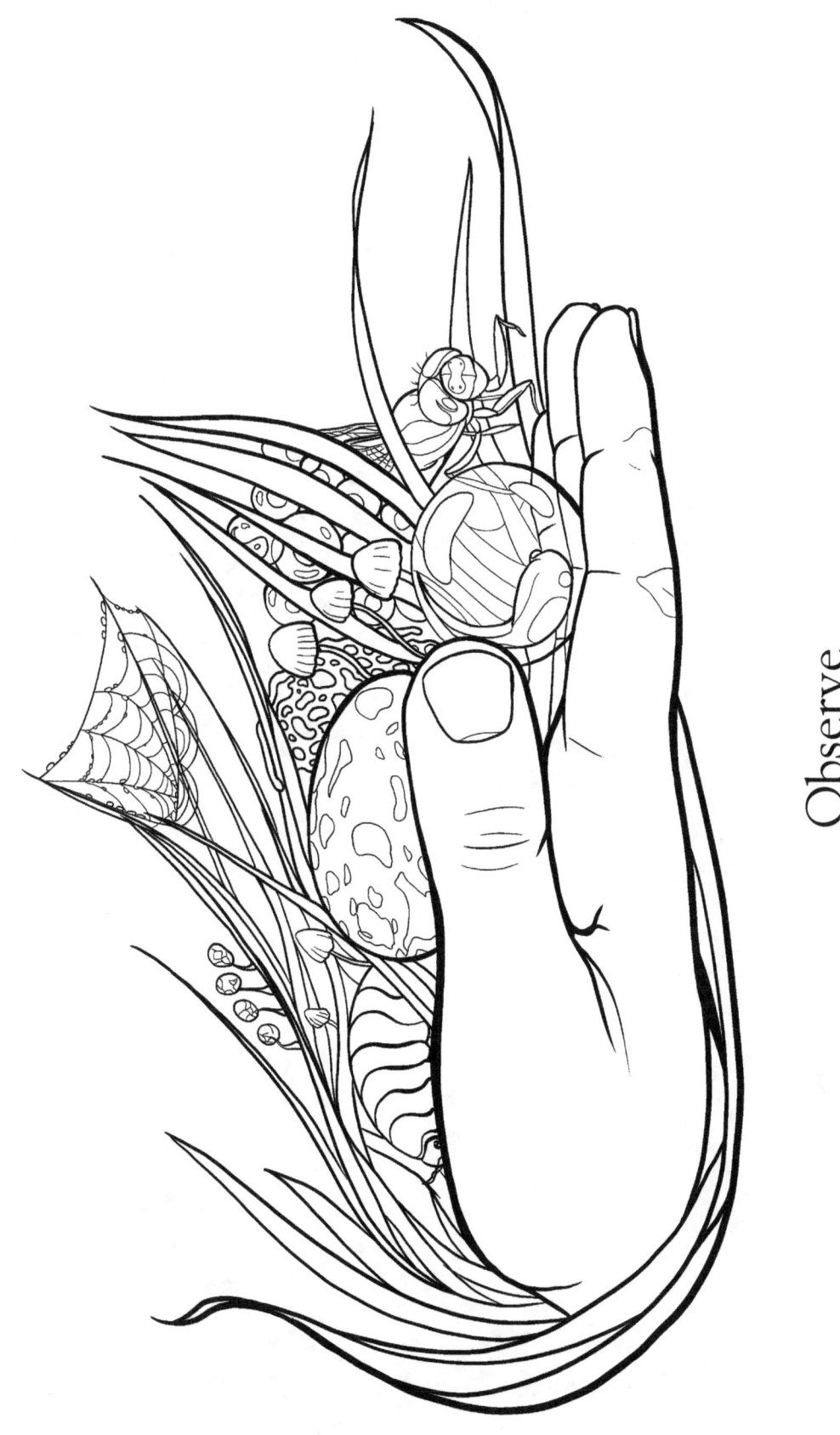

Observe

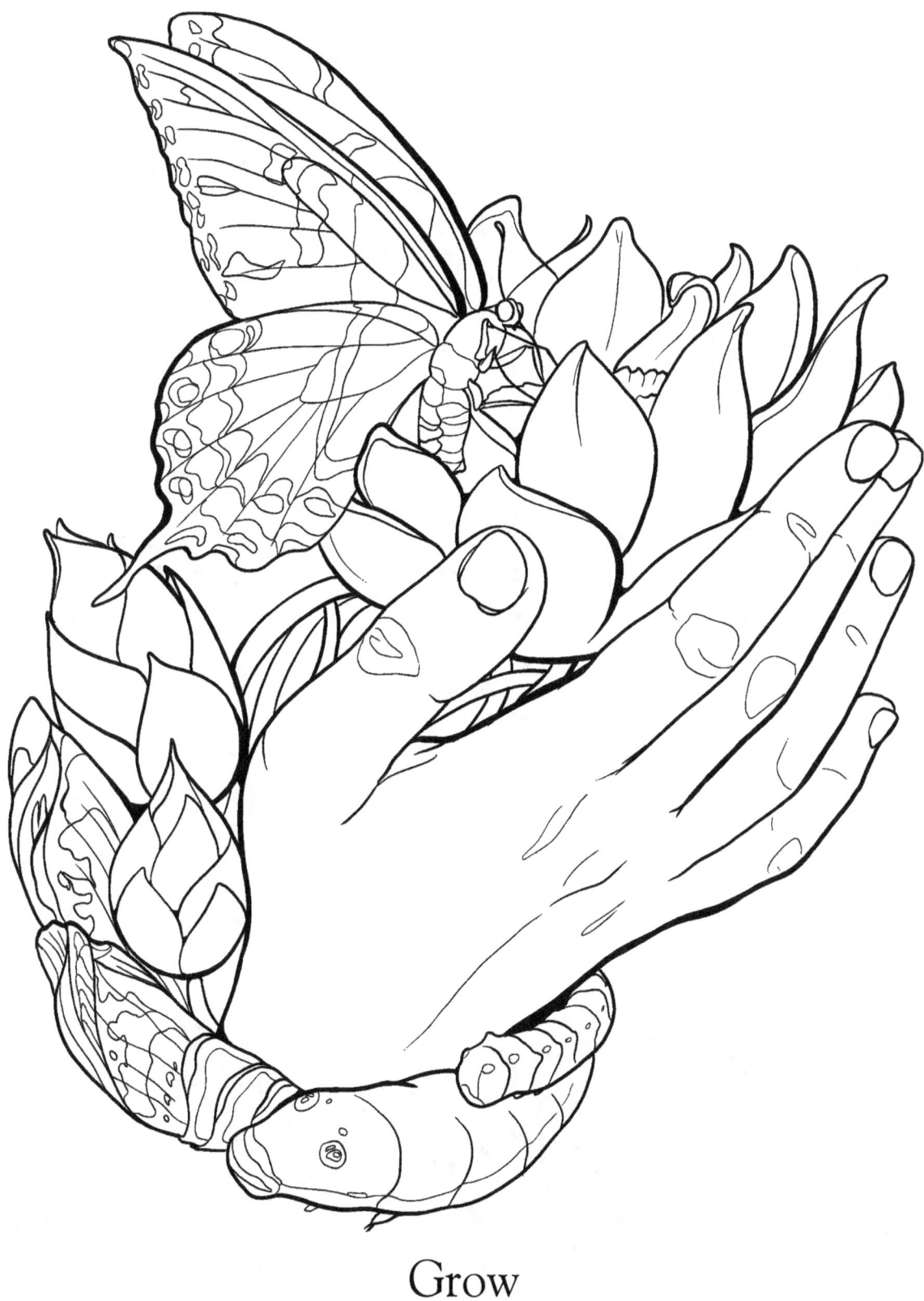

Grow

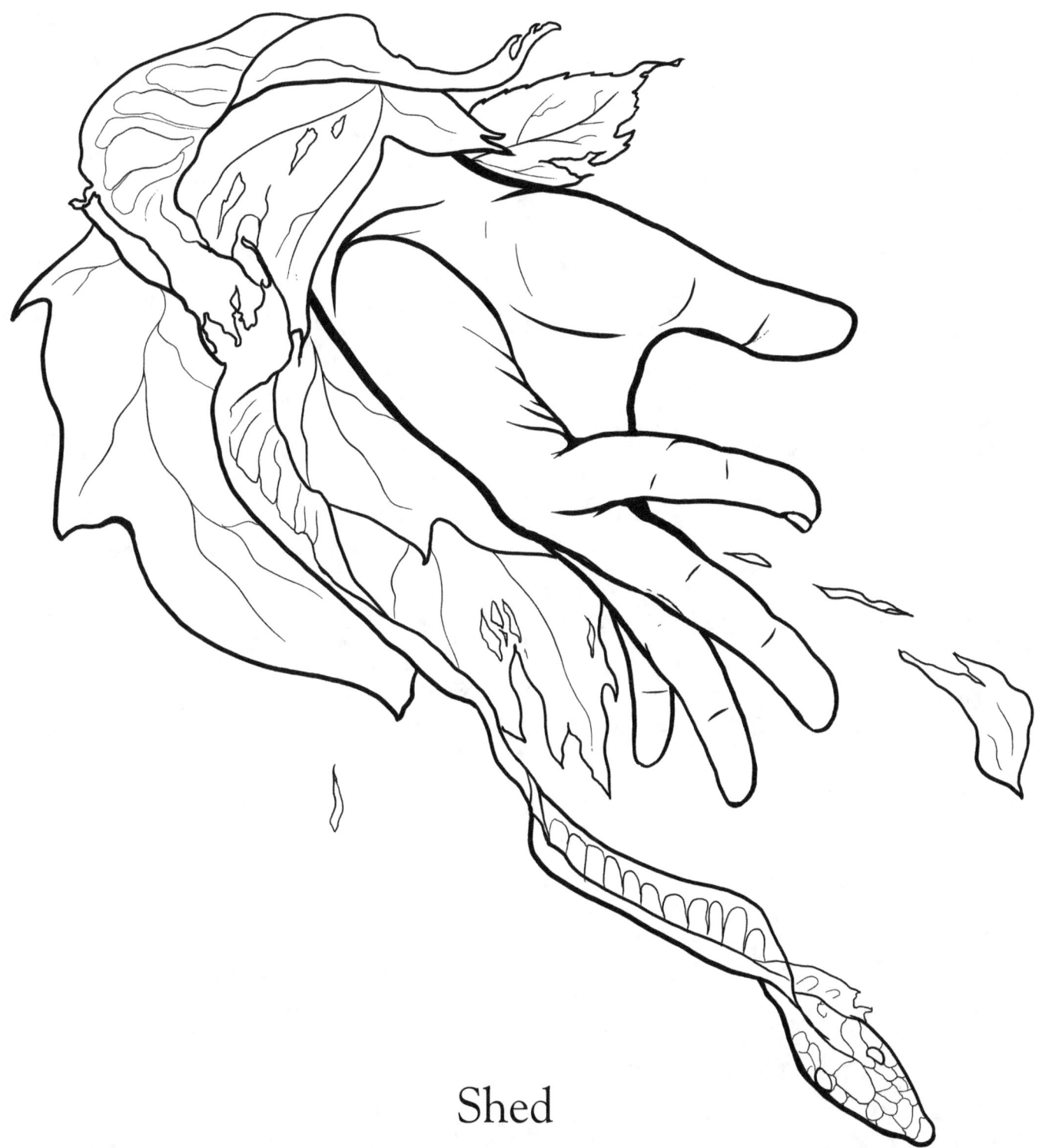

Shed

Transformation Activities

1. Go to a green space and notice as much as you can. What is in the space? What kind of plants and animals are there? Are there people there? Write or draw your observations below:

2. Return to that space a day, week, month, or even a year later. Notice at least three things that have changed during that time. Why did they change?

Observe

Spot ten differences between the drawings below.

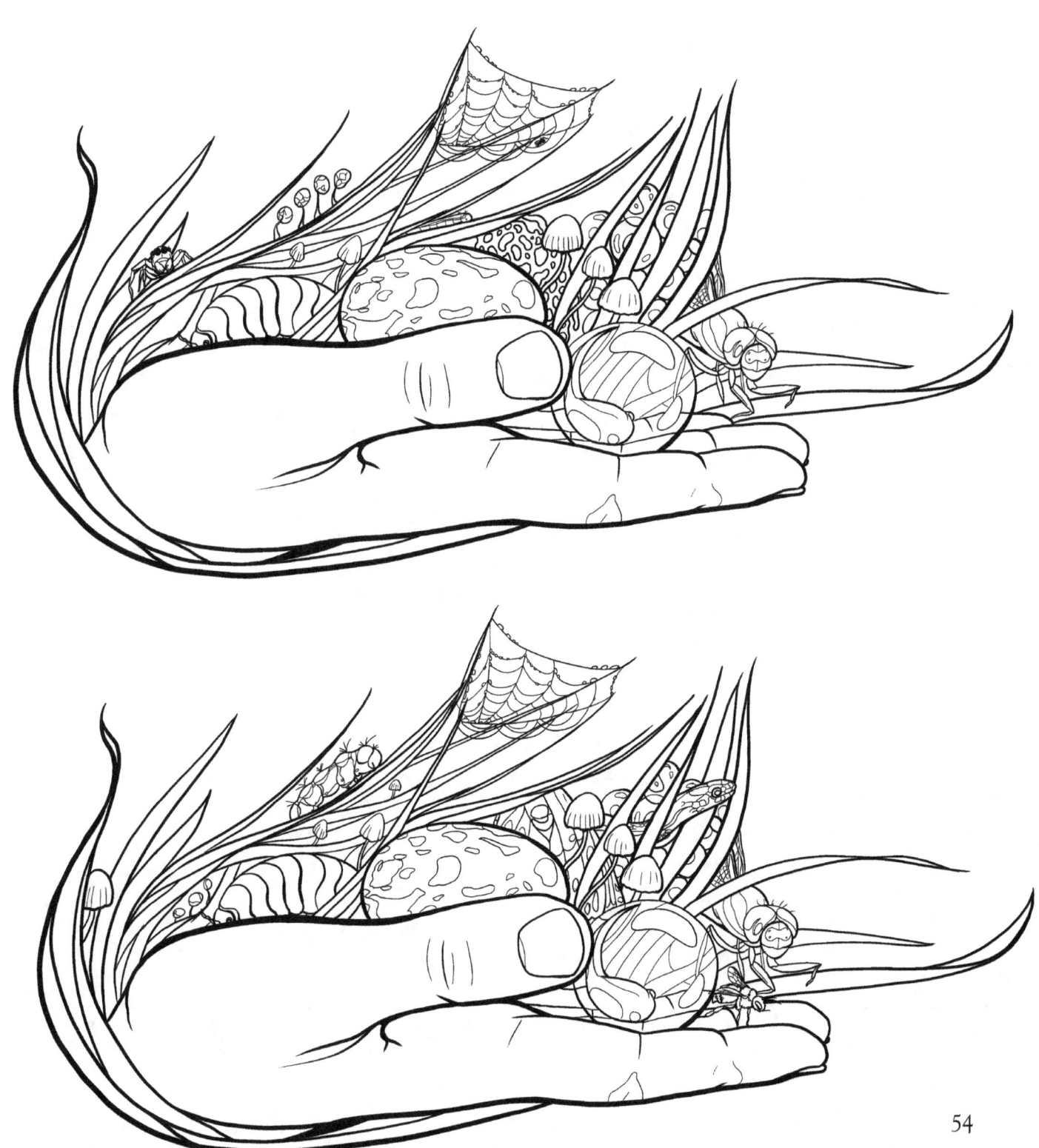

Grow

Trace the dotted lines below. Notice the shapes you've made. Build off of the drawing by repeating these shapes, until the entire page is filled (or you just feel done.)

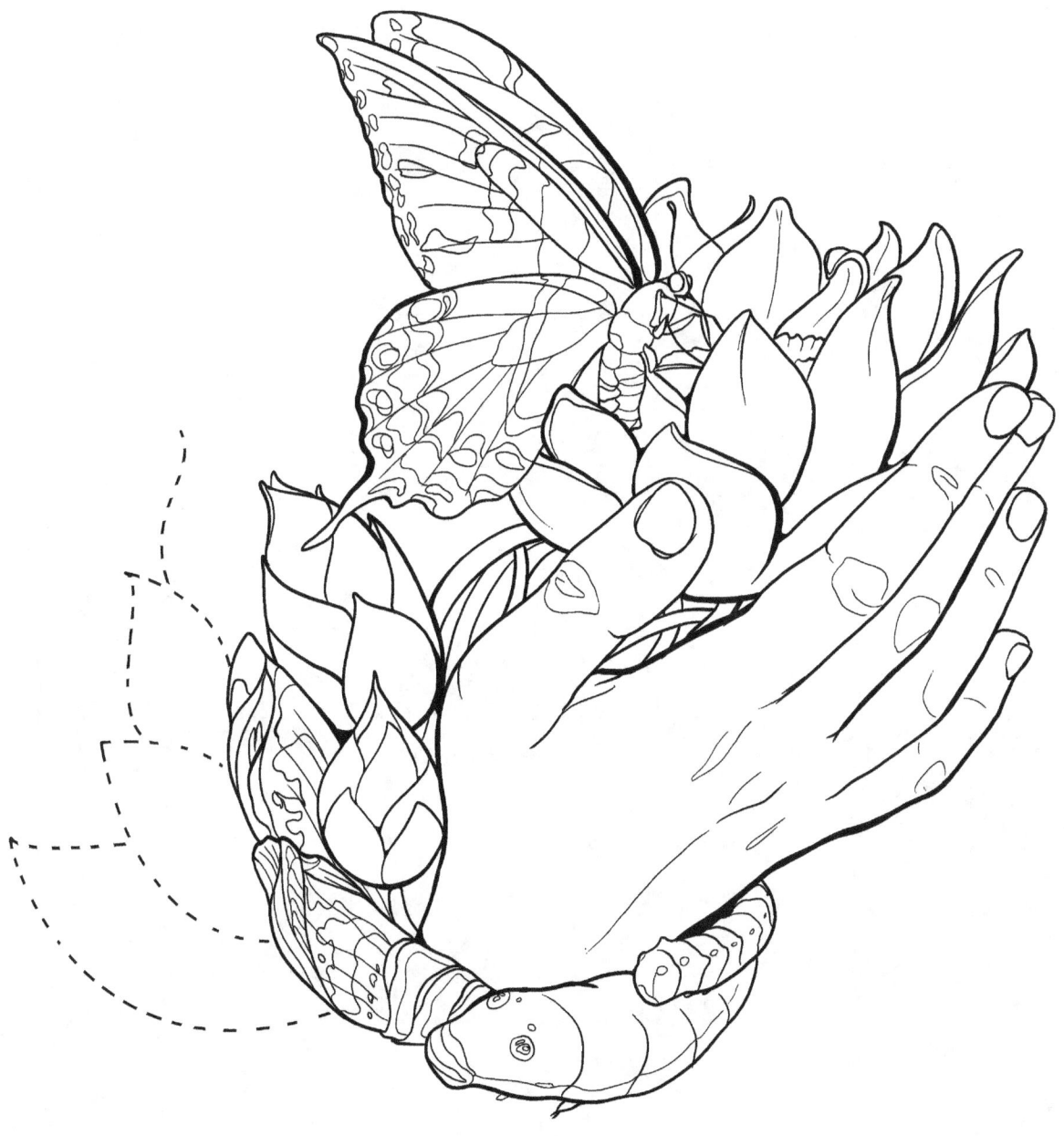

Shed

Connect the dots below in pencil. Then choose a part of the drawing to erase and color in what remains.

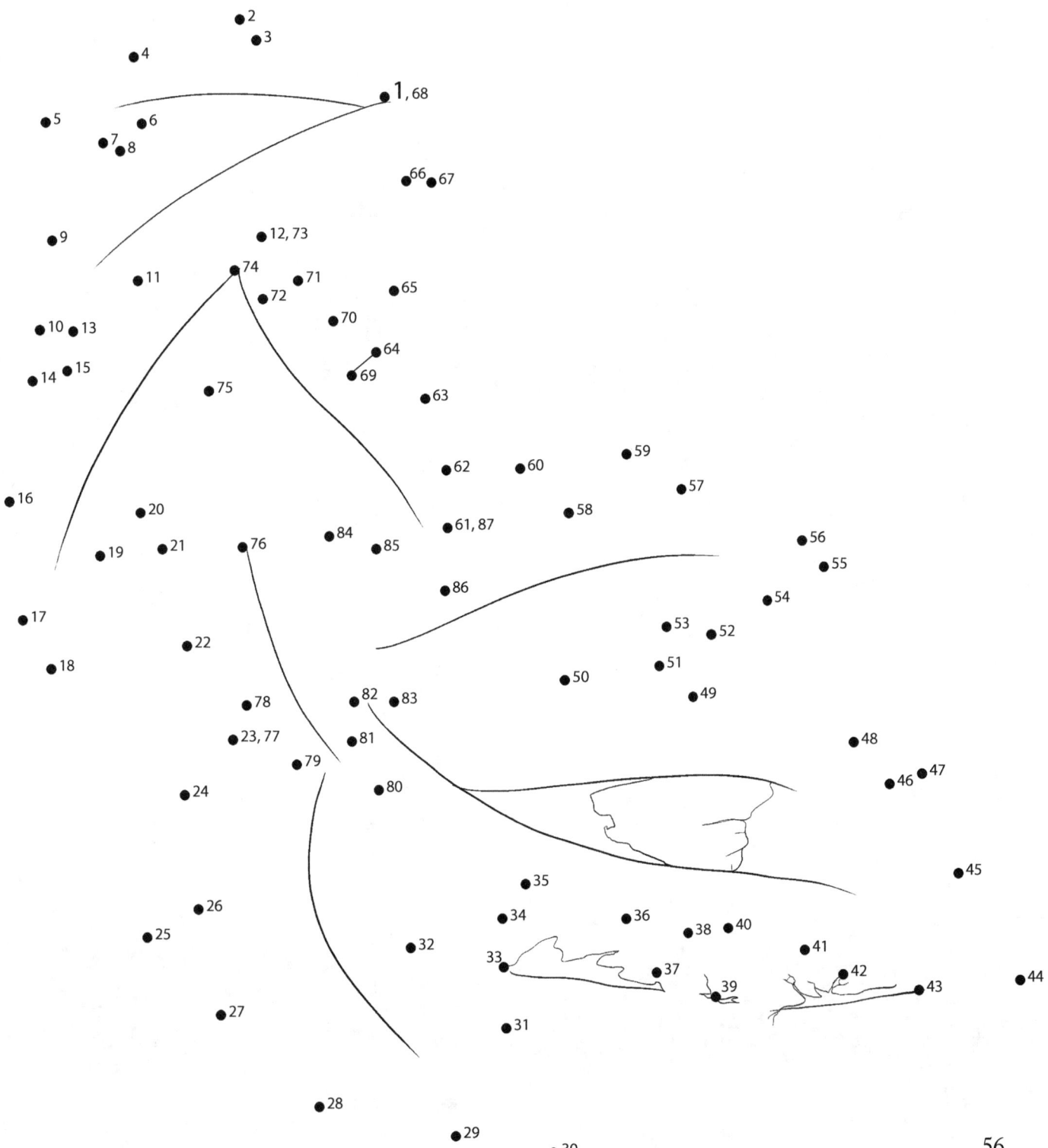

Perspective

You are not alone. You have historical, biological, and cosmic context.

In 1968, a photograph was taken of the earth rising over the surface of the moon. The cultural impact of this photograph was deep. There we were, all our passions and problems and differences and similarities, put into perspective. The ability to see the planet at a distance led to a cultural sense of earth as a shared identity and experience, one that had the potential to override differences in nation, race, and culture.

Perspective in time is also powerful. The creatures here are all early marine life, dating from the Ediacaran era to the Cambrian and into the Ordovician era. It was during this time that life went from primarily unicellular organisms to a diverse range of multicellular species, including representatives of all modern animal phyla.

Perspective for the future is valuable as well. An understanding of impermanence, both of our own selves and of other things, can be a powerful force in shaping what is important to us and what we choose to do with our lives.

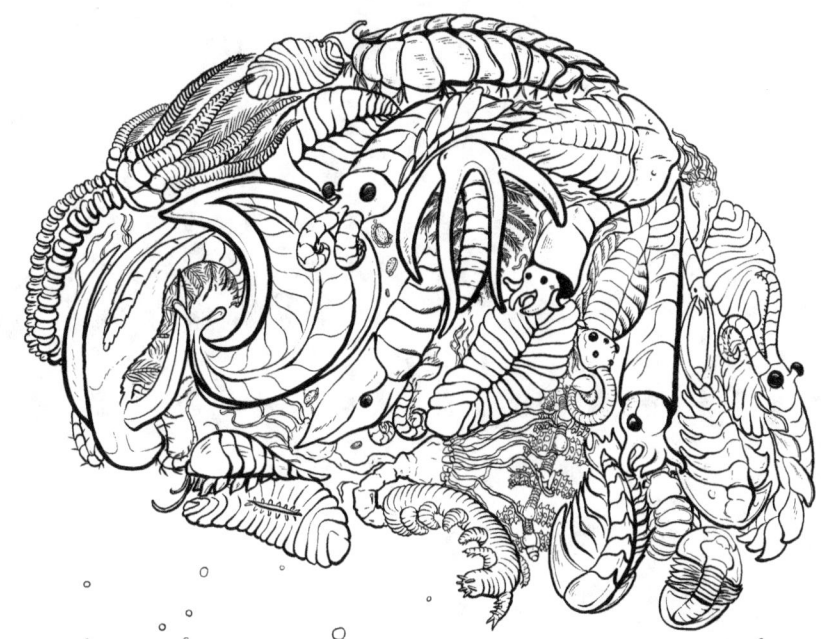

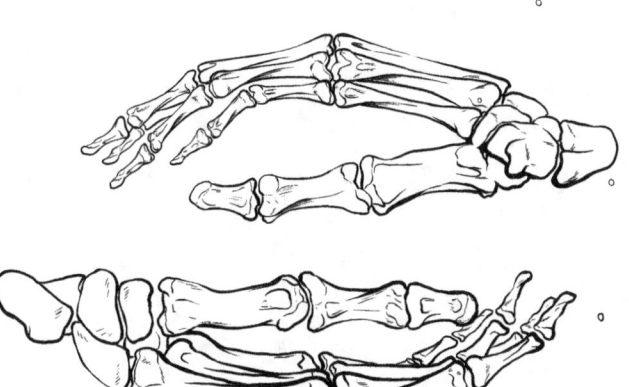

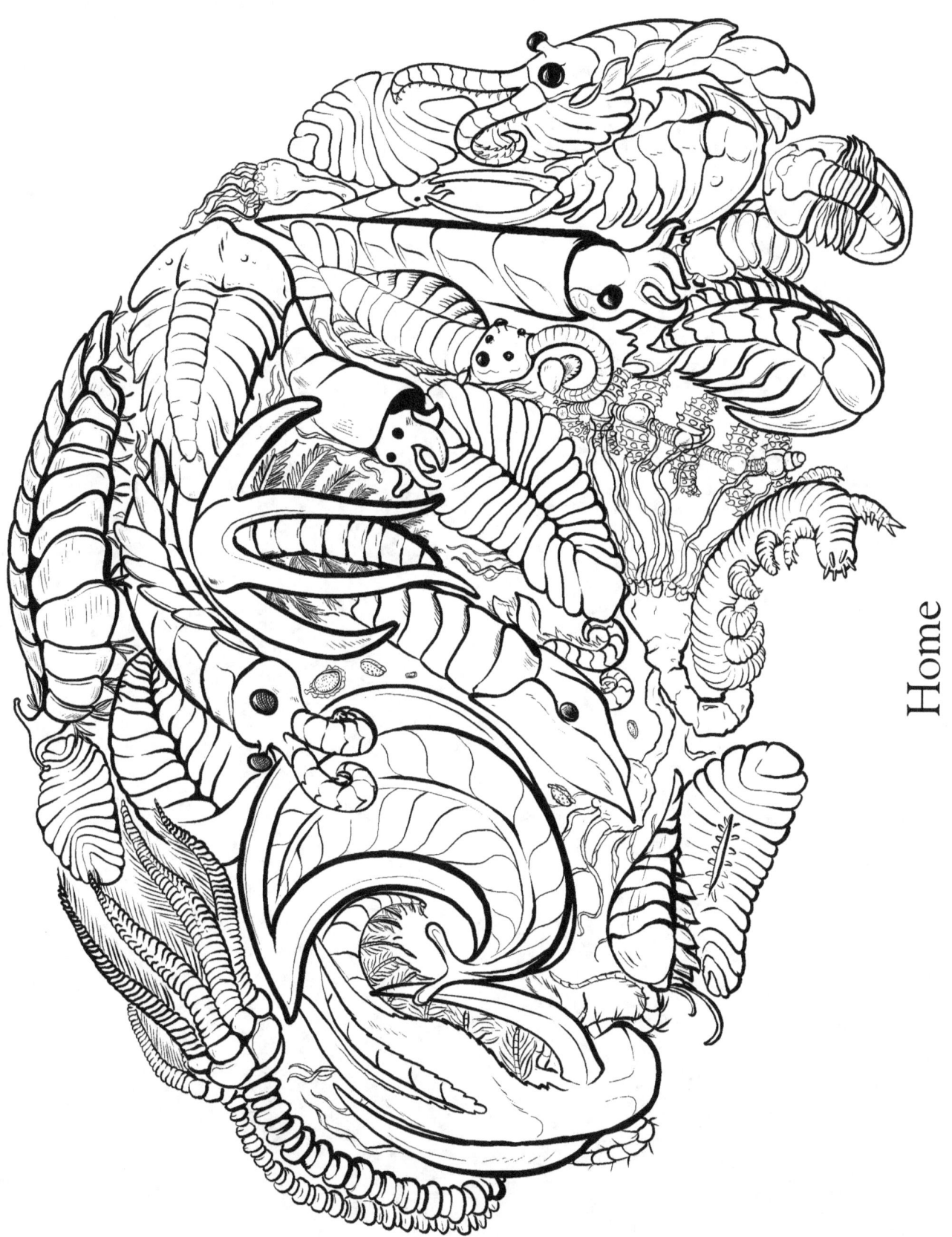

Home

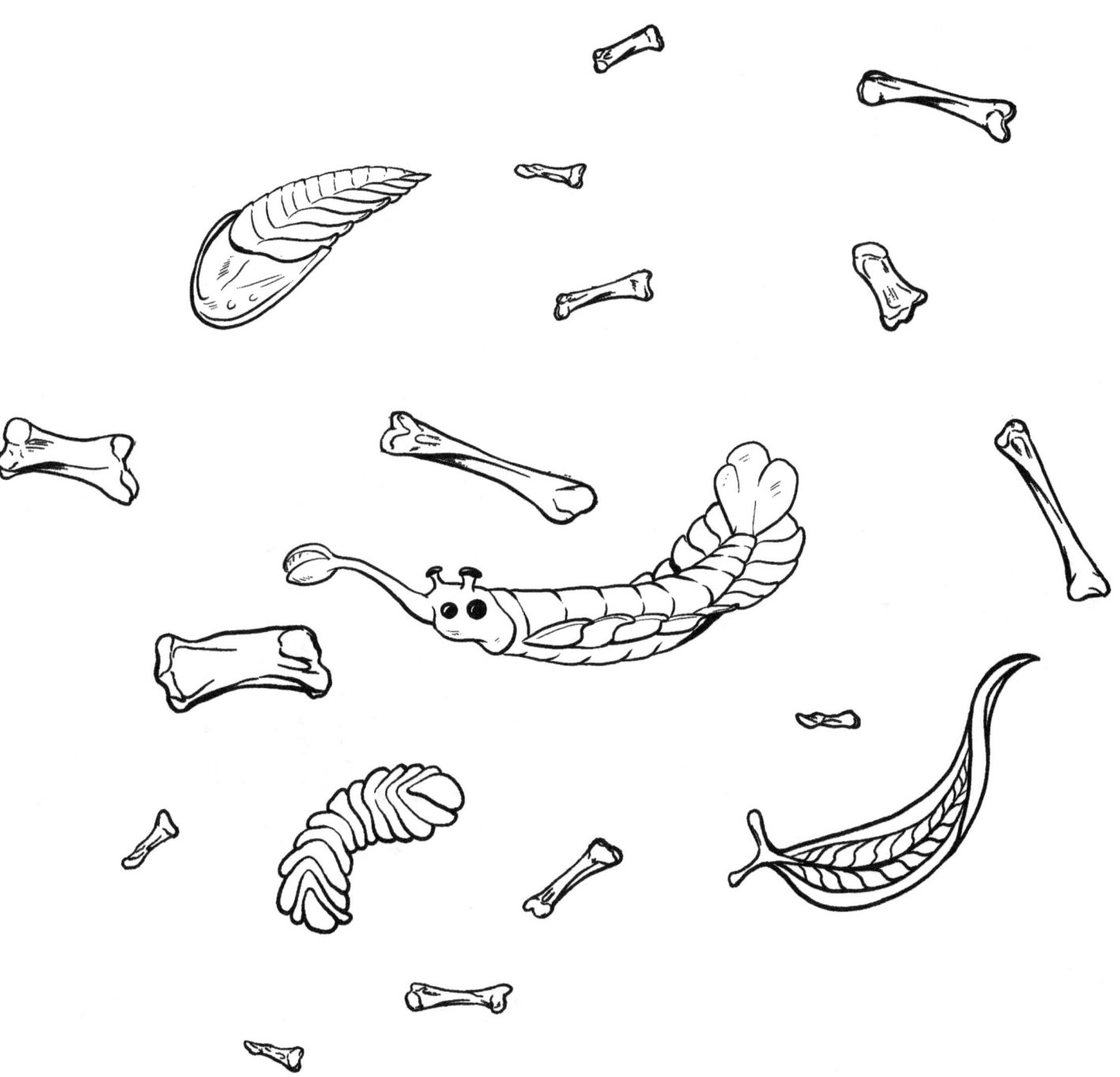

Impermanence

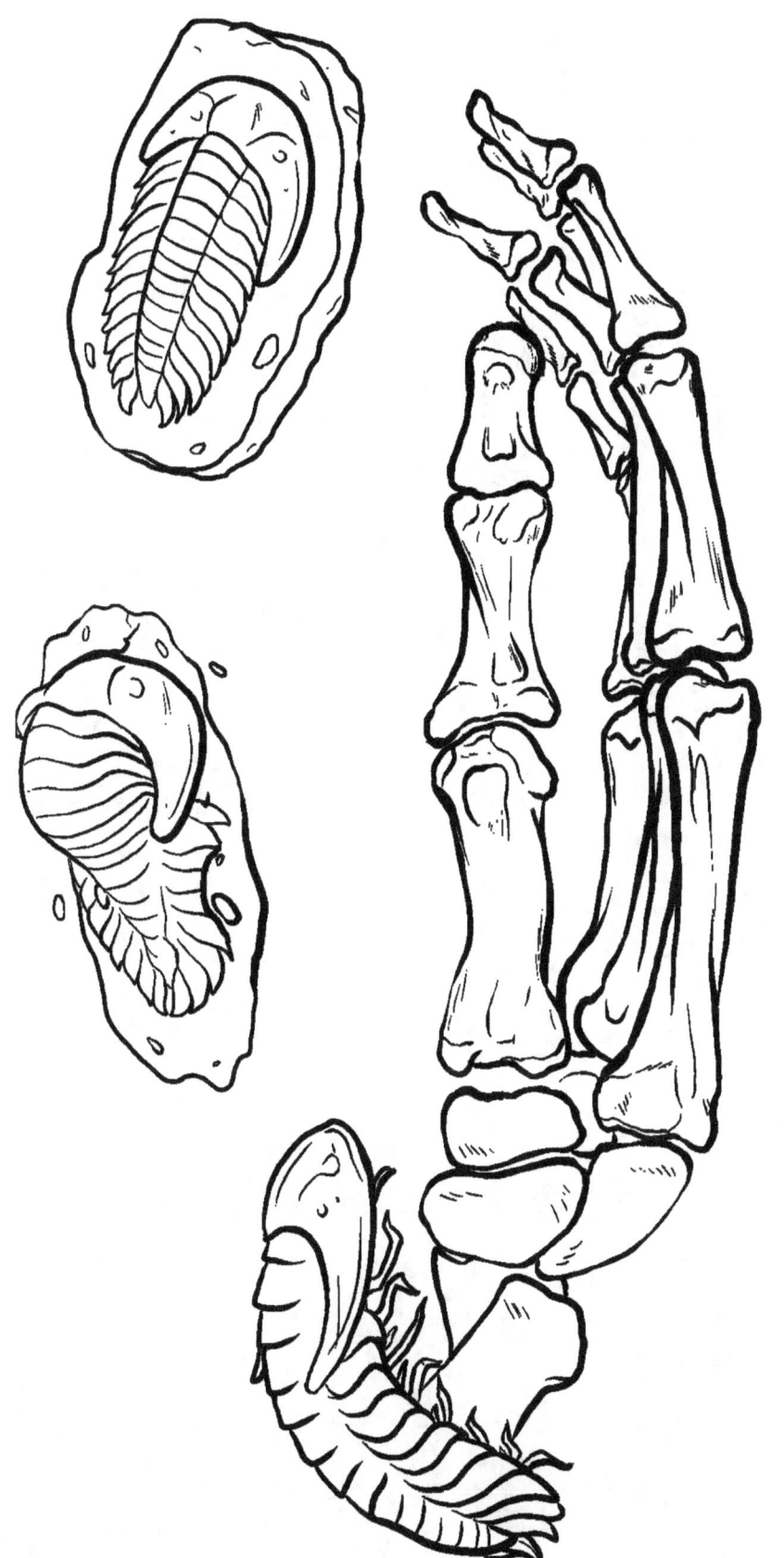

History

Perspective Activities

1. What parts of your own history do you know? Draw or write something from your history below. It could be a family story, a piece of natural history, or even something from before the earth formed billions of years ago.

2. Talk to a friend and share memories about your home towns. If you don't have a home town, share a memory about what feels most like home right now.

Home

How many of these early forms of marine life can you find in the image below?

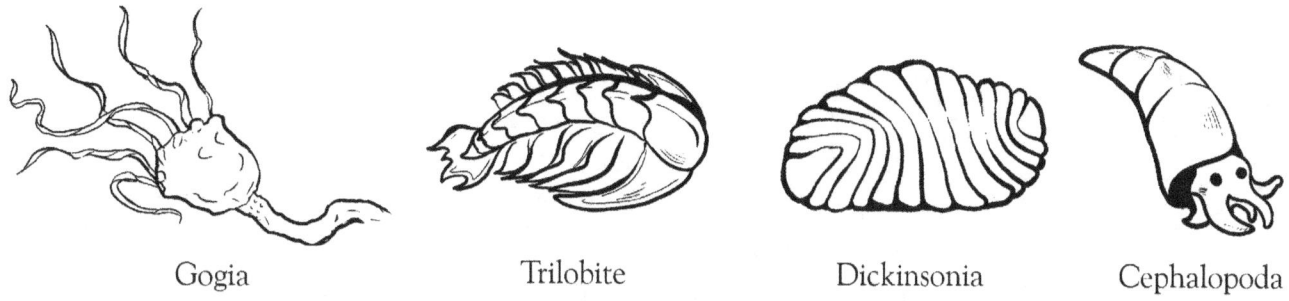

Gogia   Trilobite   Dickinsonia   Cephalopoda

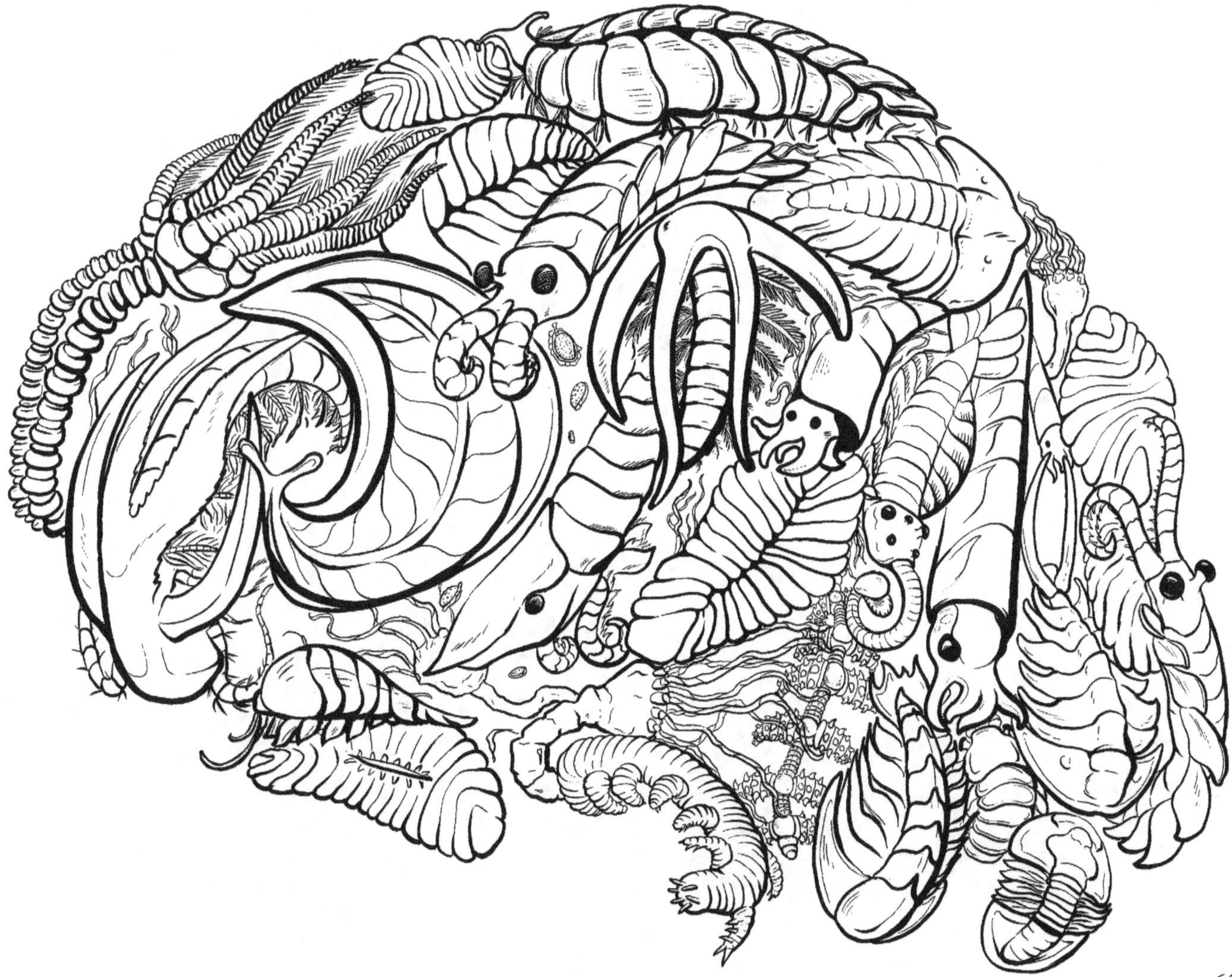

Impermanence

Connect the dots in pencil, then erase.

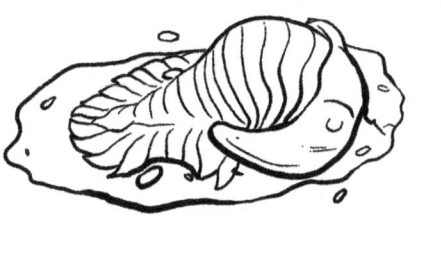

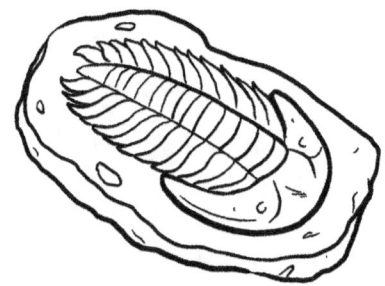

History

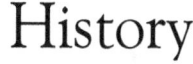

Make a drawing in pencil below. Erase the drawing. Notice the faint lines, scuff marks, and other history that was left on the paper. Make a new drawing from what remains.

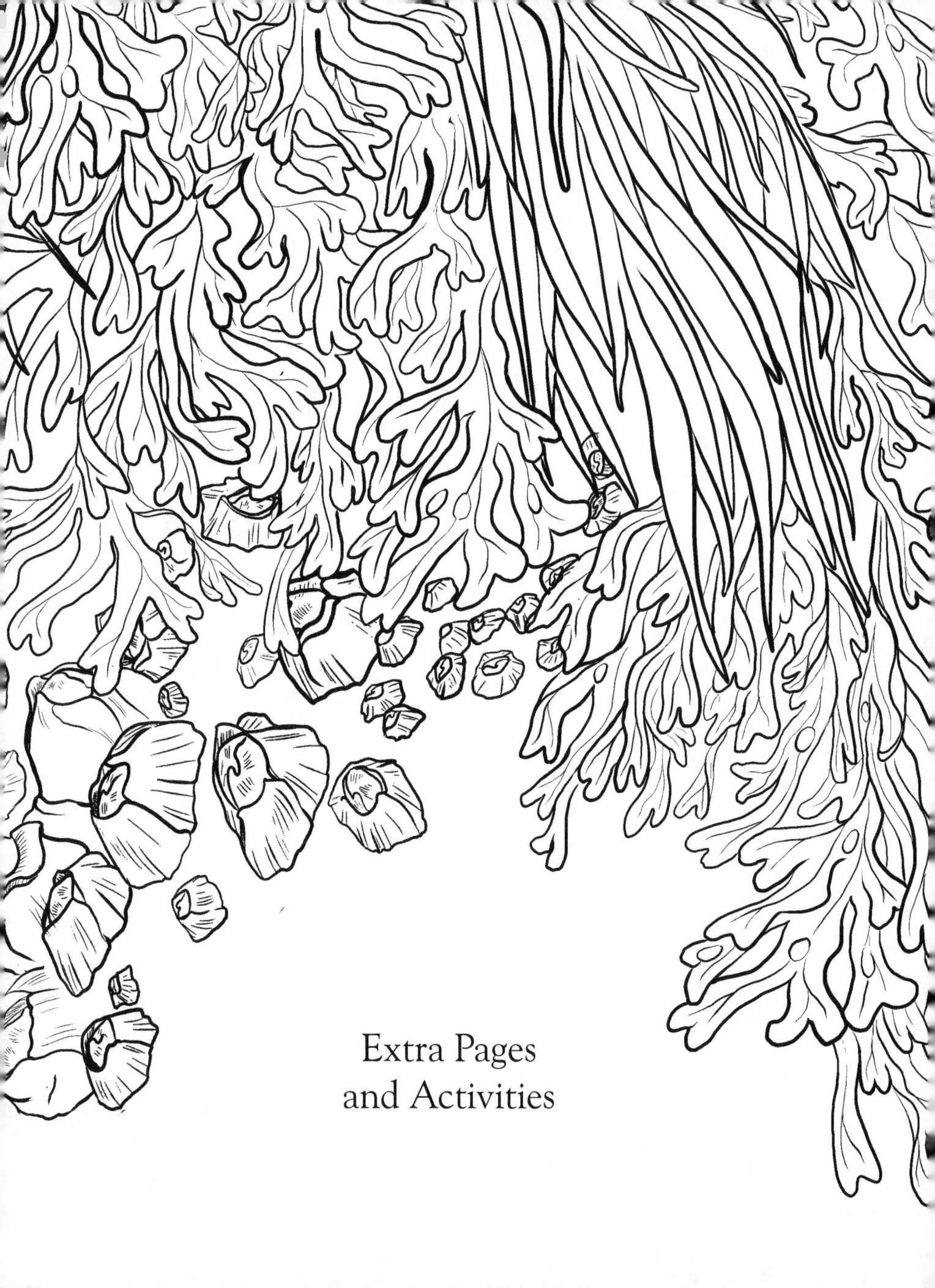

Extra Pages
and Activities

Seven Strengths
Word Search
(easier)

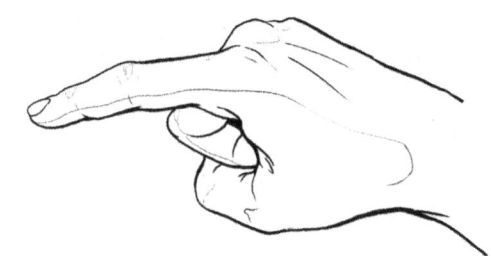

```
S T R A N S F O R M A T I O N C R A L H P T T B O
V X G C P W Z L R W C O E L X H W R B P R Y Y O G
L M S O A N S F A A C O M M U N I C A T E Q X T C
Z M B K E M N C C M M Z A N I C B T E V A N G E R
W J P H C Z M Z P X B N H X T V T Q C Q L V Z F K
K W E O G R Z P R K H O R F P B V S I H K A O Z C
I H R L X T A U E A A E Y P A R U U M G G W L H C
Z Y S D L O R Z S M O Q I A E C O M P A S S I O N
E L P T O D E S I R E Y N B N U Z O E W Z Y N M J
I N E I Y K N X L S U T S Q I C W W R F I D M E X
A S C G I Y C R I H O R U Y R G Y A M H D G R O W
V B T H X E P V E Q B H L E C O L L A B O R A T E
N N I T F P U C N J S P G R S M T Y N B H T X T I
R U V H E H T D C L E B V U B E H H E L G R F C D
E P E W K I D K Y S R D D Q I V E G N D X H J E K
S S Z D A K C S O L V E C J X H C K C F C V T B C
P H S B B R I V I M E R V Q Q S V P E S F Q N V X
E Y M W L Q N M N Y J W P O S Z D D U H R E T A T
C V L L P A S S I O N T S T A T T R A C T E P K R
T B D C H D I N C R L E V H E O H I S T O R Y E F
P V G L E A G L S A N P Z X F D Y J Z T V X K V
R B O A O P H G I H D W W F X D H D F B Z F H S N
U B P U P T T V C Q R J L E T G O Q T L O V E C U
I L N G K W T M T H P D E T E R M I N A T I O N K
R A Y H C I A Y R C J T D T I S U B G L L D A A S
```

Resiliency	Impermanence	Solve	Compassion
Hold Tight	Passion	Communicate	Respect
Let Go	Anger	Transformation	Collaborate
Adapt	Determination	Observe	Flamboyancy
Perspective	Desire	Shed	Laugh
Home	Insight	Grow	Warn
History	Seek	Love	Attract

67

Seven Strengths
Word Search
(harder)

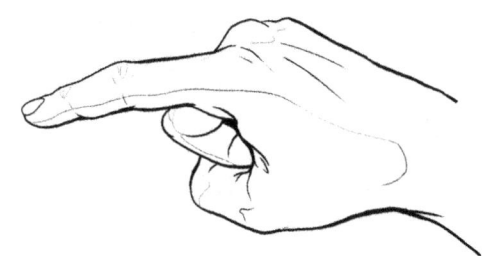

M N O I T A N I M R E T E D T Z M W O R G P N M J
P X S M F P Z U I K W T L N L J J D E Z N Y O J Q
L L V K B W T P I V S K H I S T O R Y B N U C K F
J H D N O B S E R V E F Y G Q Y W G N R A W B G D
B U G L L M E J F V L V R X I Y X U T O D X H N F
Y I G U D W J I I A B S B C J S P P K E E S E K I
F U V S C M M Q M I W Q M W Q F N Y Y G L V I Z J
M W E J O L D B Z E A N U U M Q G I L M I H Z I A
C I U V L B O P L O V E K L B C V L I T N L O Y Q
Q W K G L Y Q E E T A C I N U M M O C V S H M V N
D N J J A O I Q T Z C R M I W Y L E I U X X T O J
Y G E N B Q S M X H D E S I R E P W U W H X I A W
X O C S O K X H P Q X G P Z L S U N L N I S W W S
I Y F D R Z R D K E L N A S R V O N H H S L X A P
G U L E A W S V Q B R A T E E I V I L A Z S W D L
T T A H T T E I A A T M P S S R V K P M O Z D A O
A F Q S E B C W P G C T A S O Q K A B K Z E U P Q
Q T I M R F Q B H E I Q A N I L K L M D W G M T L
I M T E I N X A D O X P L N E C U A Q B H W V O D
K W M R O N J T E P M V C W M N I P M V L B K R H
T N Q L A T D Y M O D A H Y F K C L H E H O F V W
T C A Q T C A M C T M R E S I L I E N C Y Y O K X
W N F N P V T W G L S N E W I Q S Q A P D R V V
D H Q E I T H G I T D L O H B E H W G W I W S K U
Z K Z K M N R J X U Y S B C I Q K W B P S Z E O P

Resiliency	Impermanence	Solve	Compassion
Hold Tight	Passion	Communicate	Respect
Let Go	Anger	Transformation	Collaborate
Adapt	Determination	Observe	Flamboyancy
Perspective	Desire	Shed	Laugh
Home	Insight	Grow	Warn
History	Seek	Love	Attract

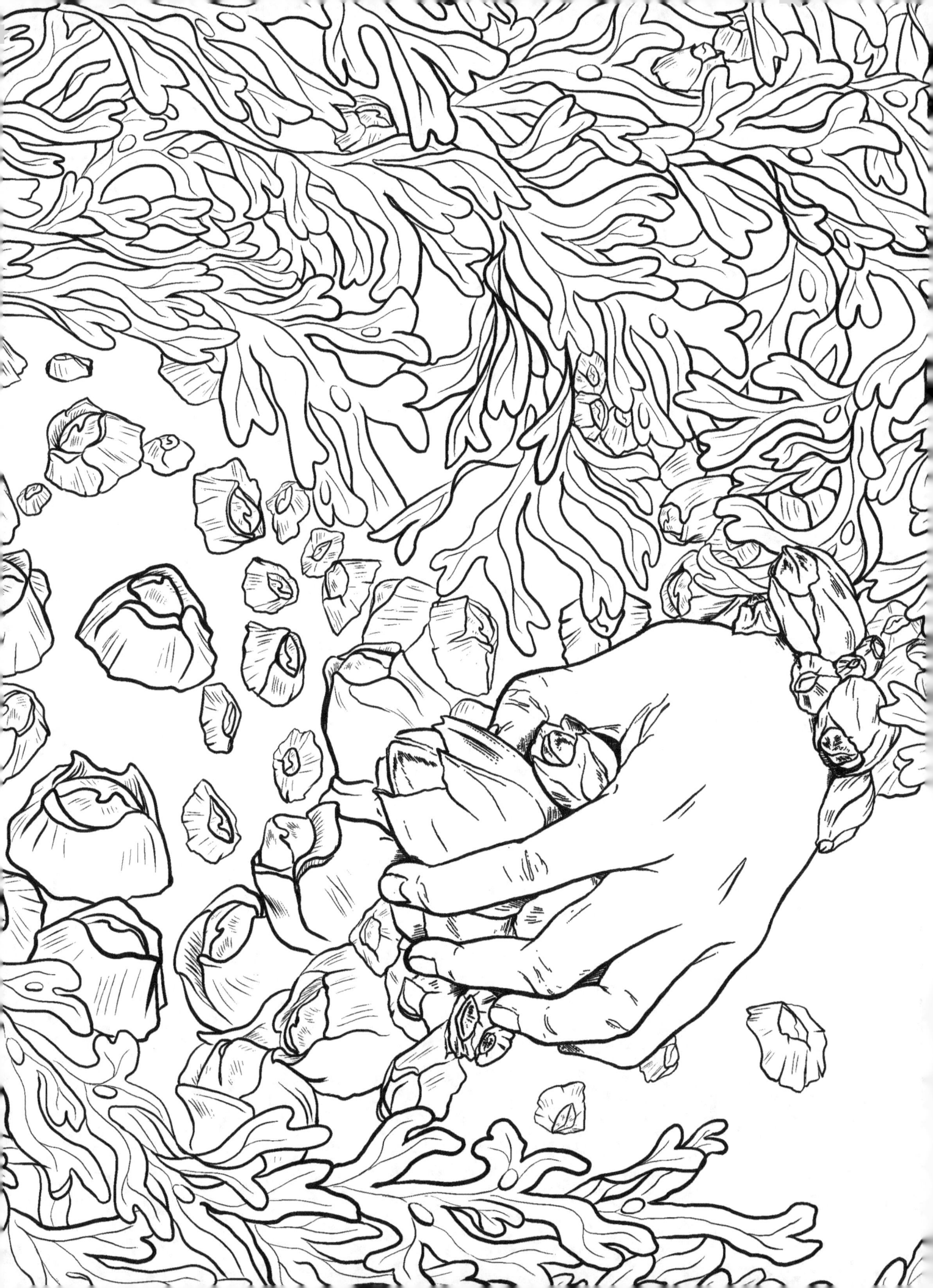

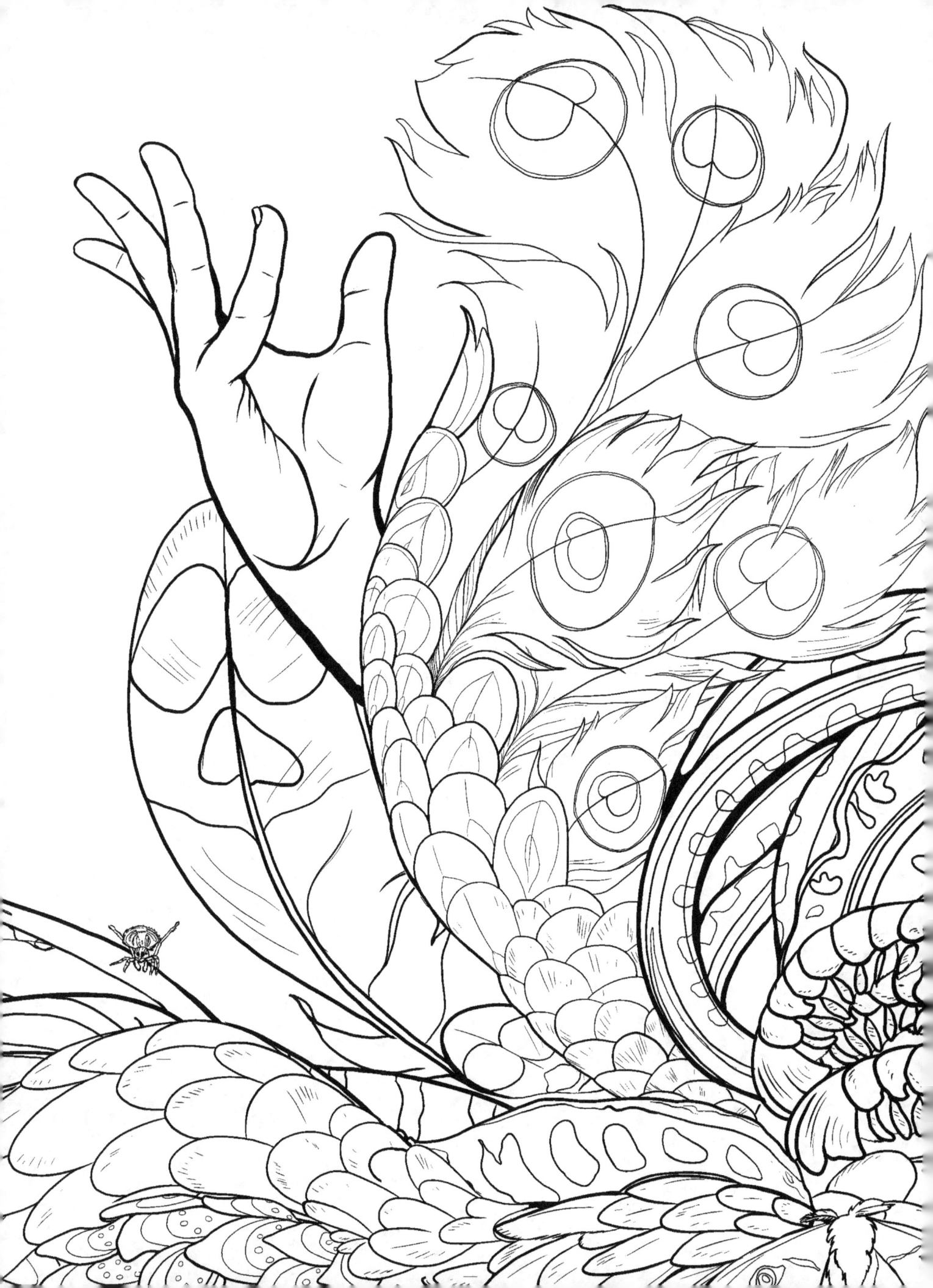

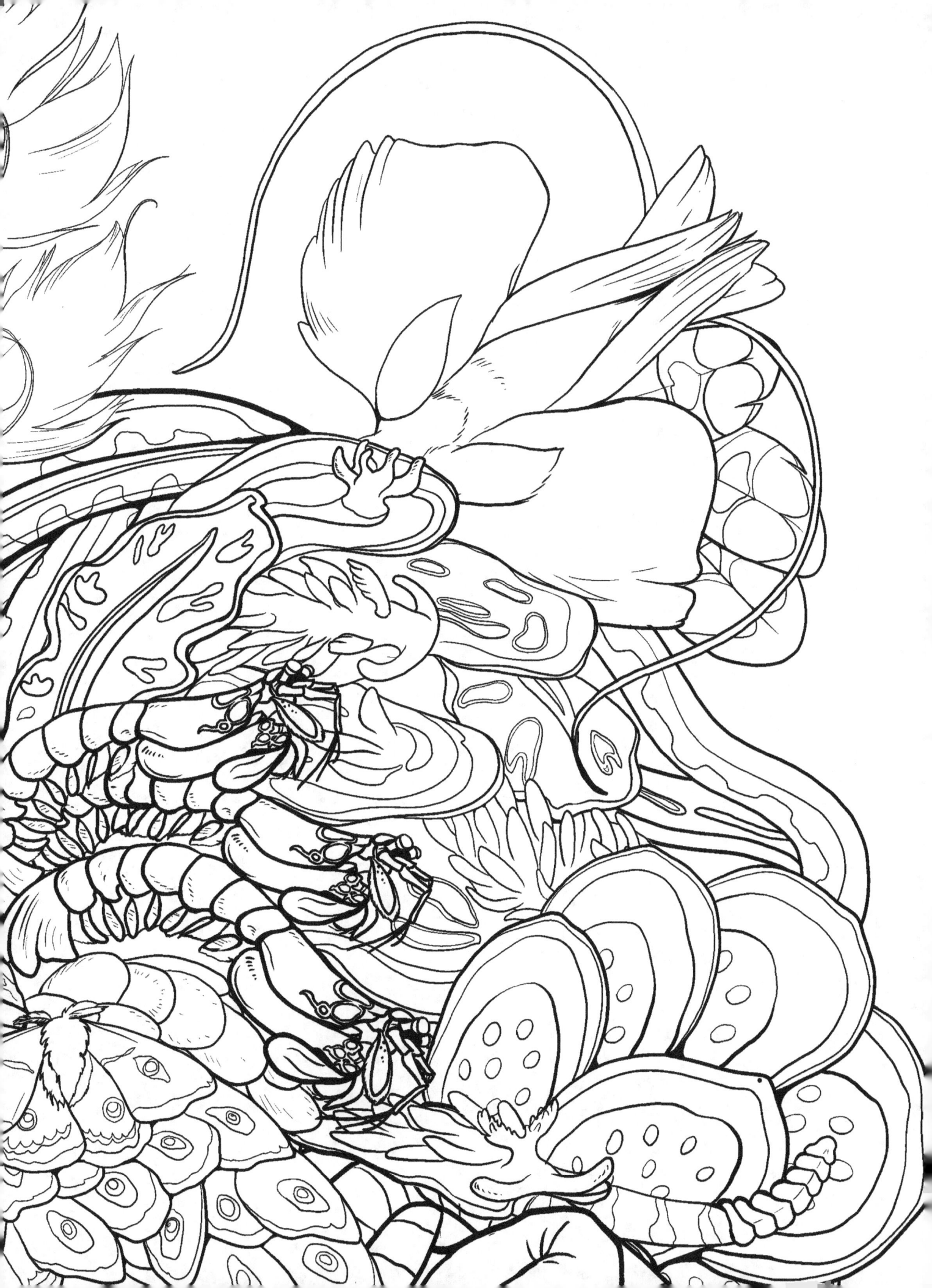

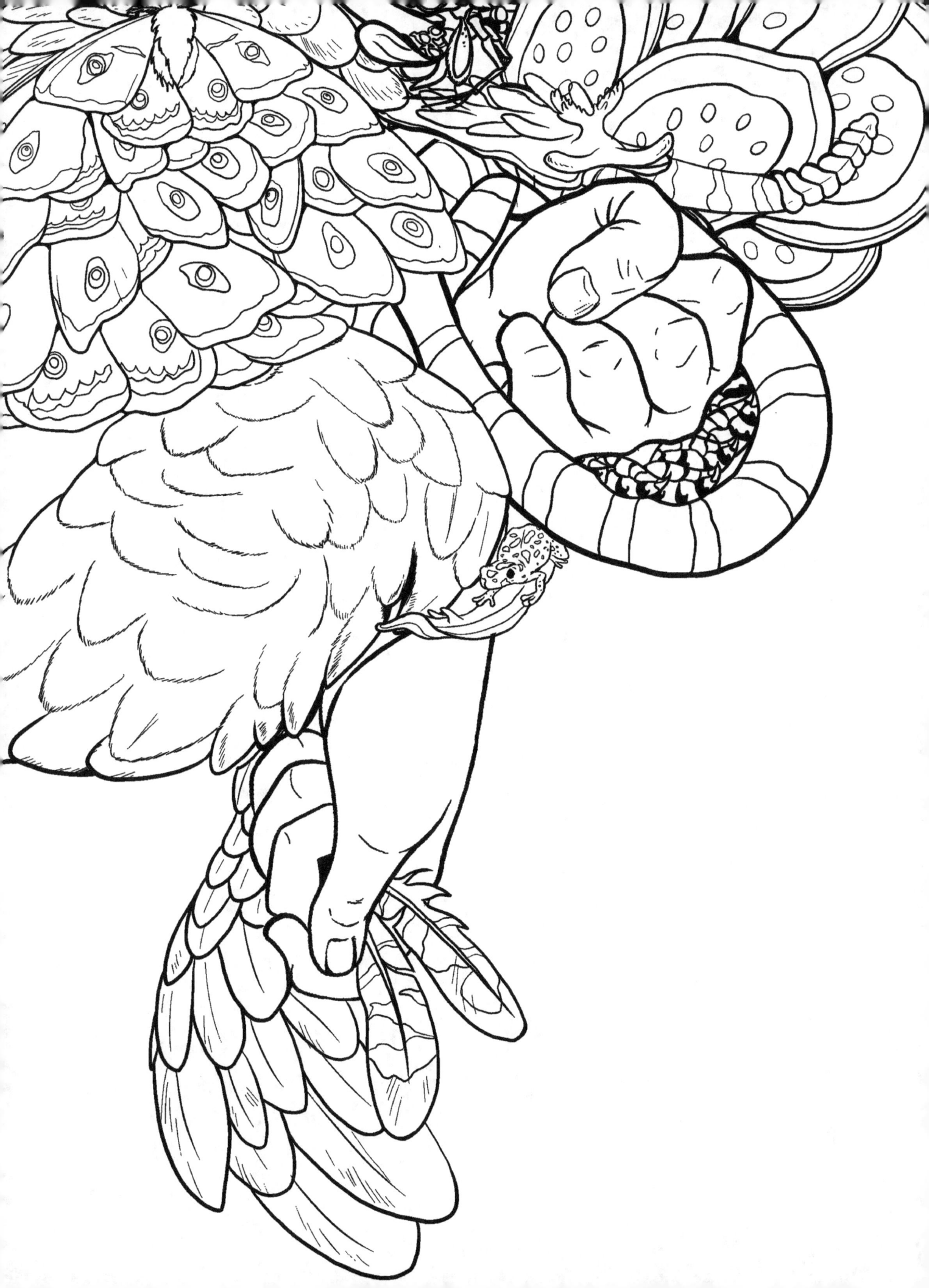

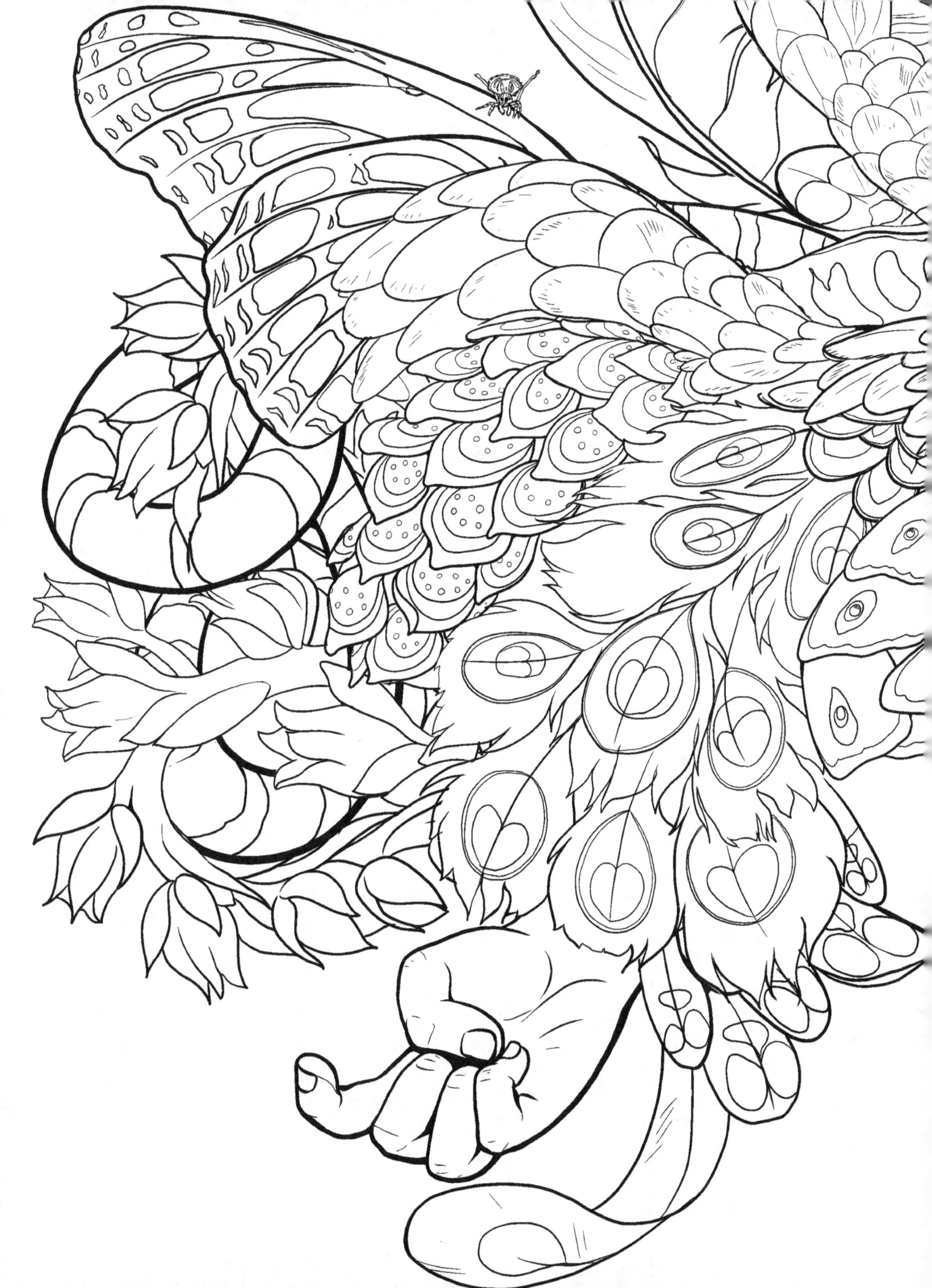

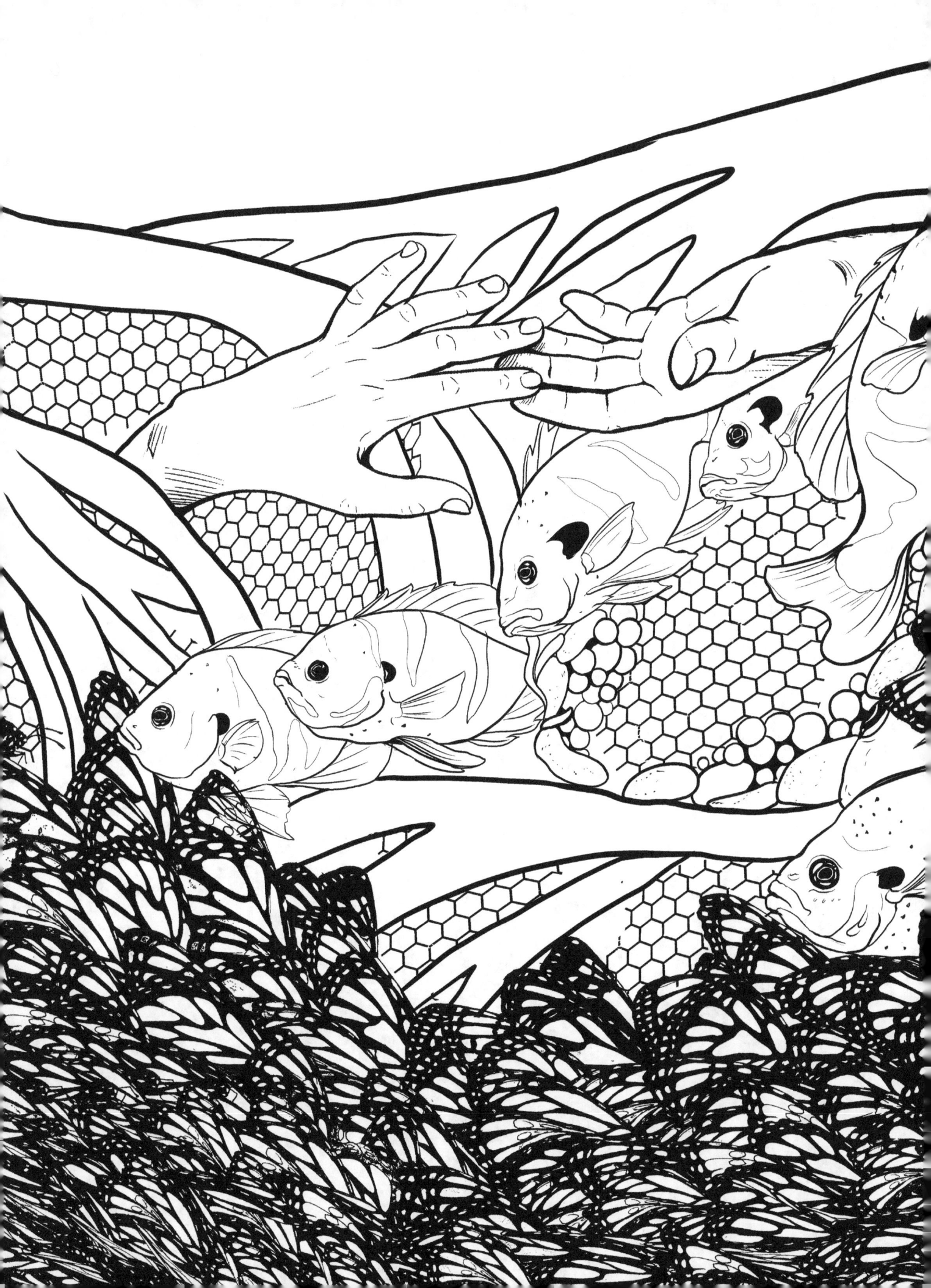

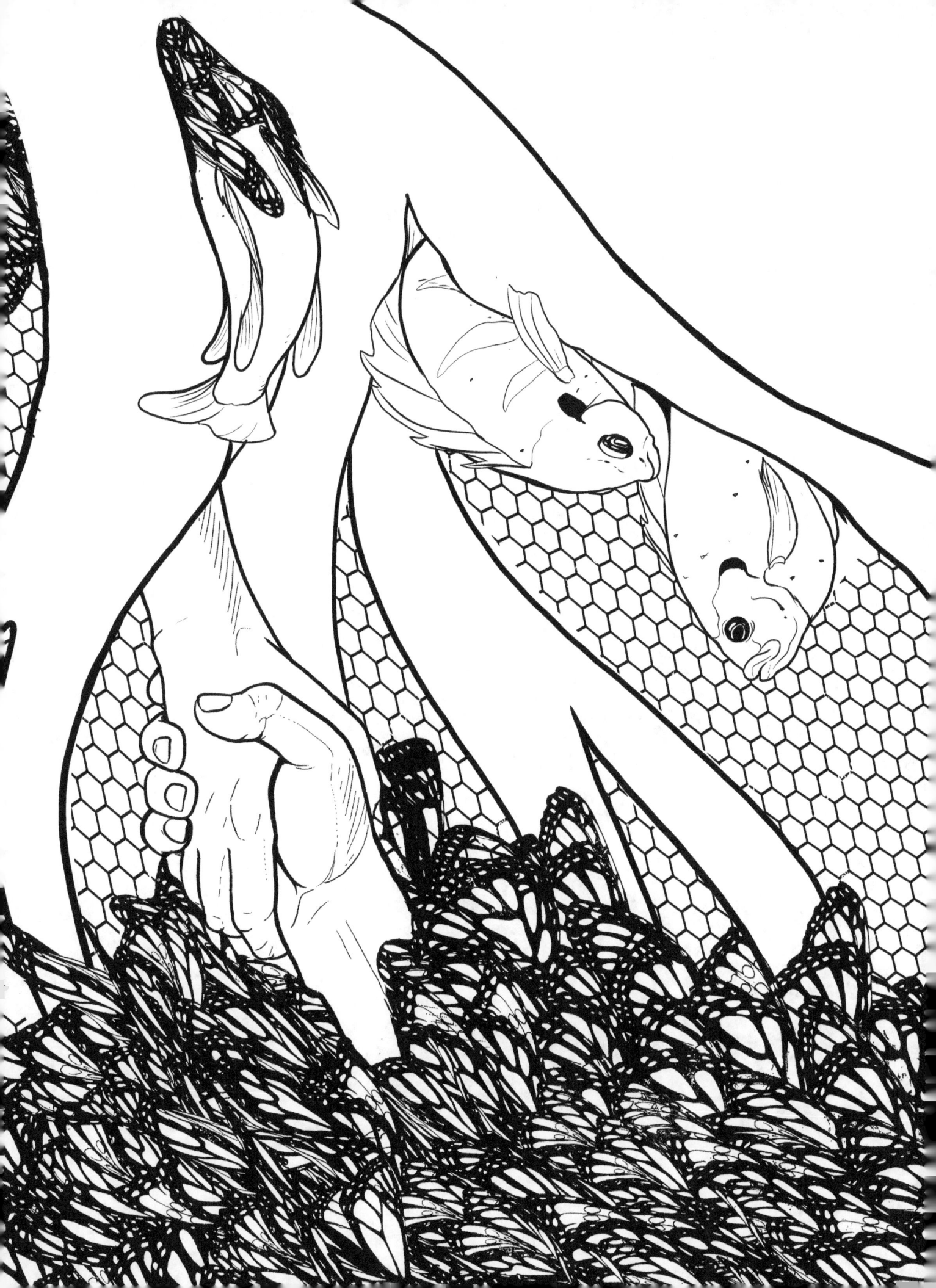

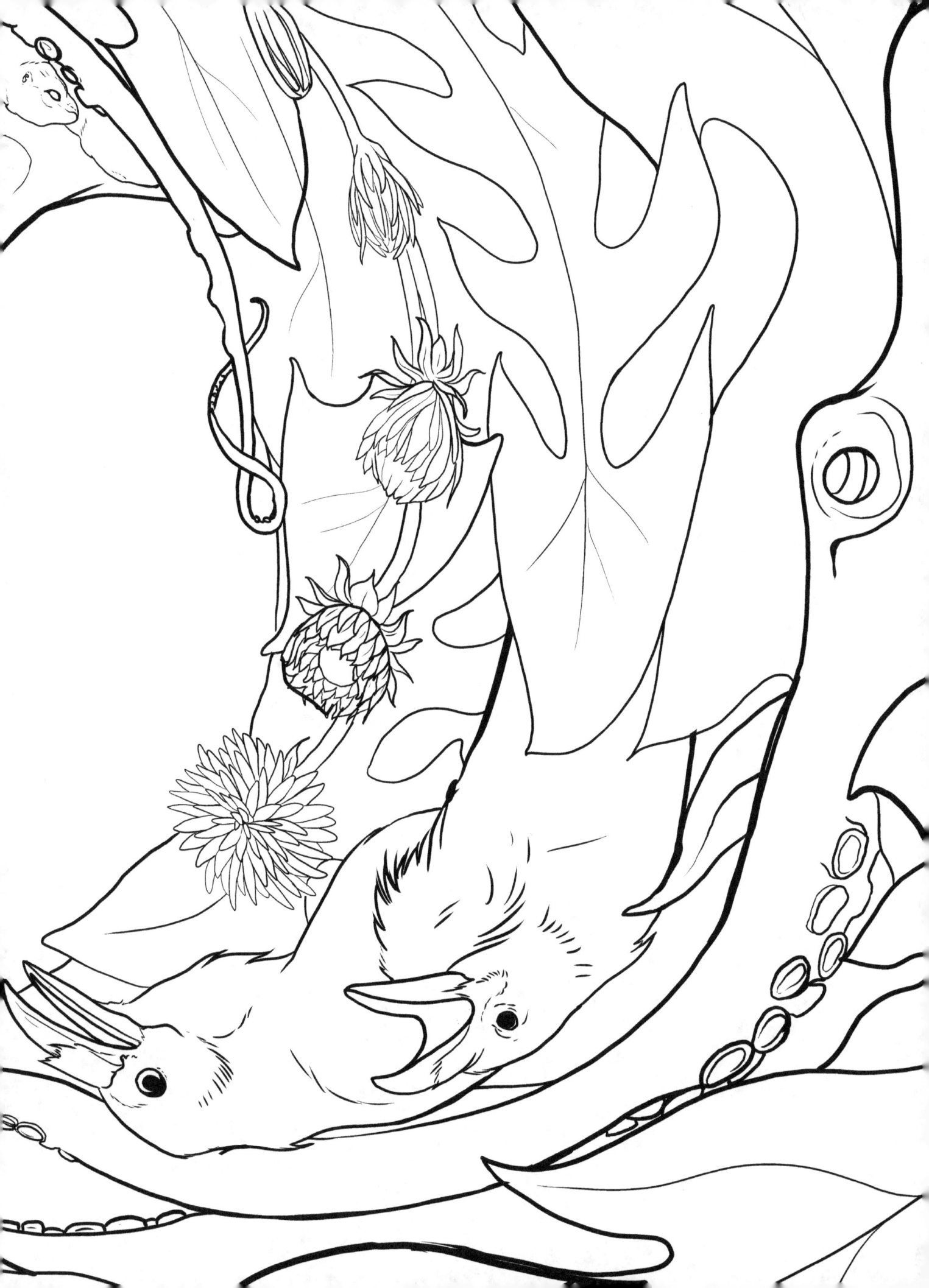

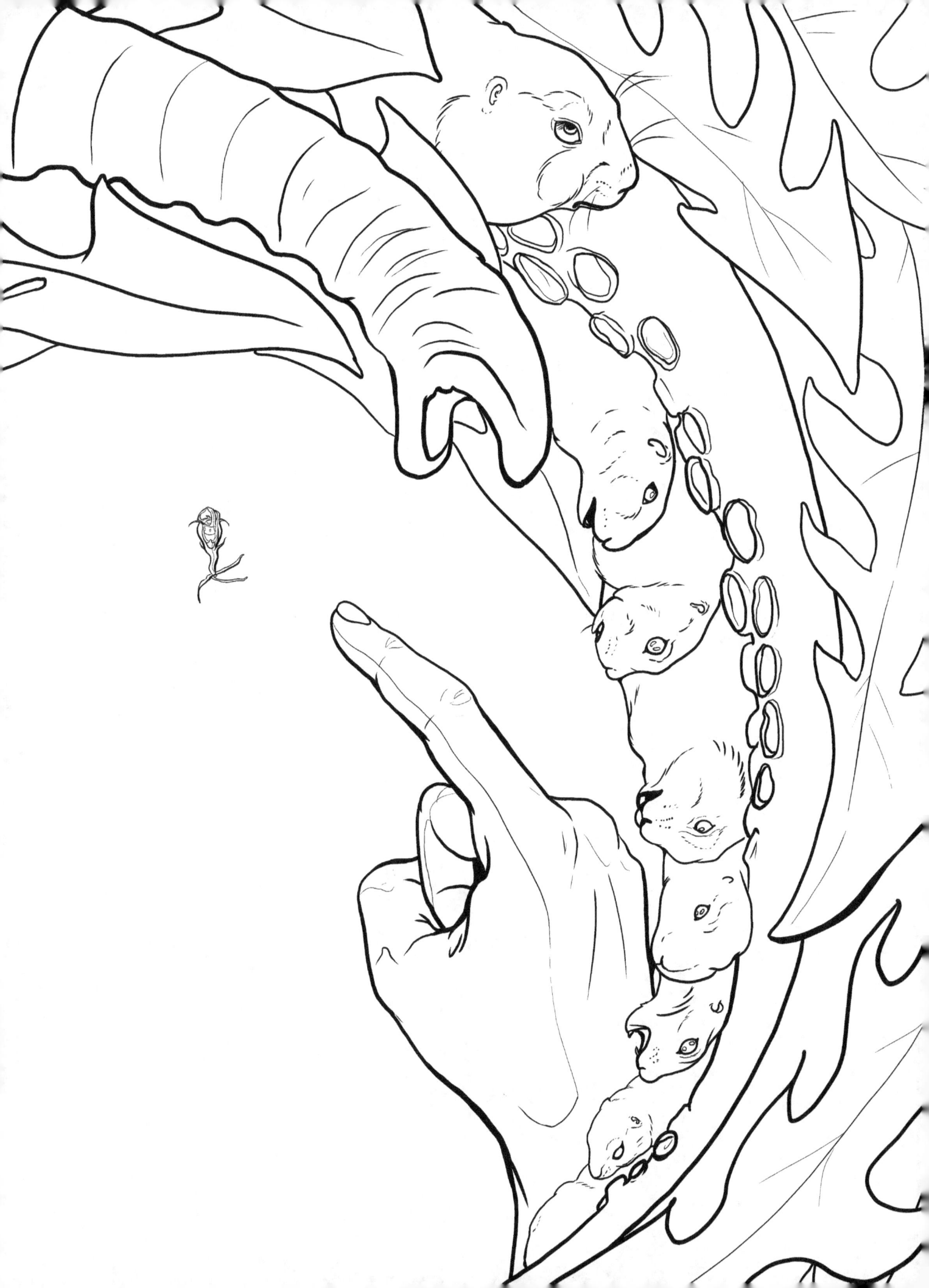

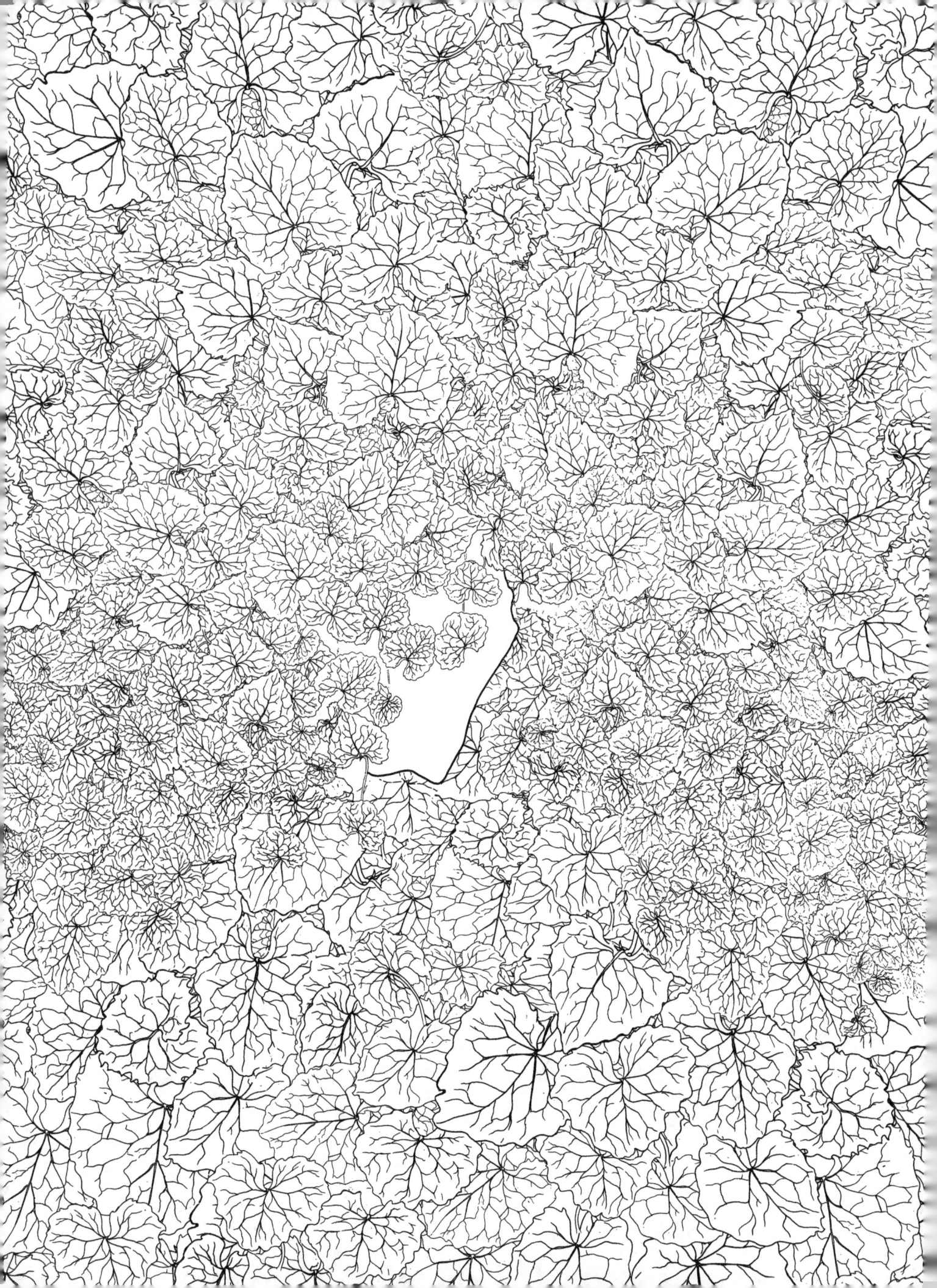

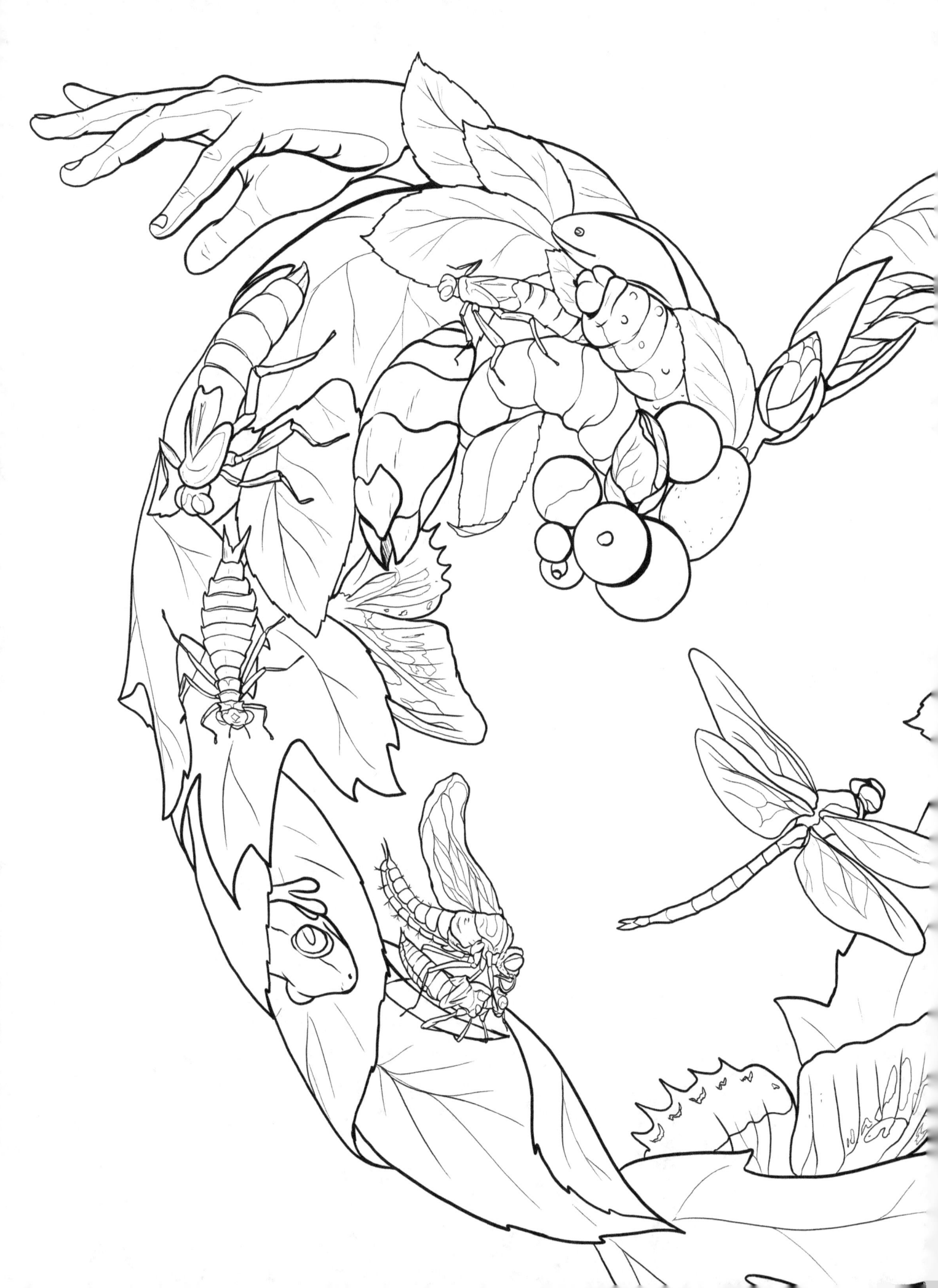

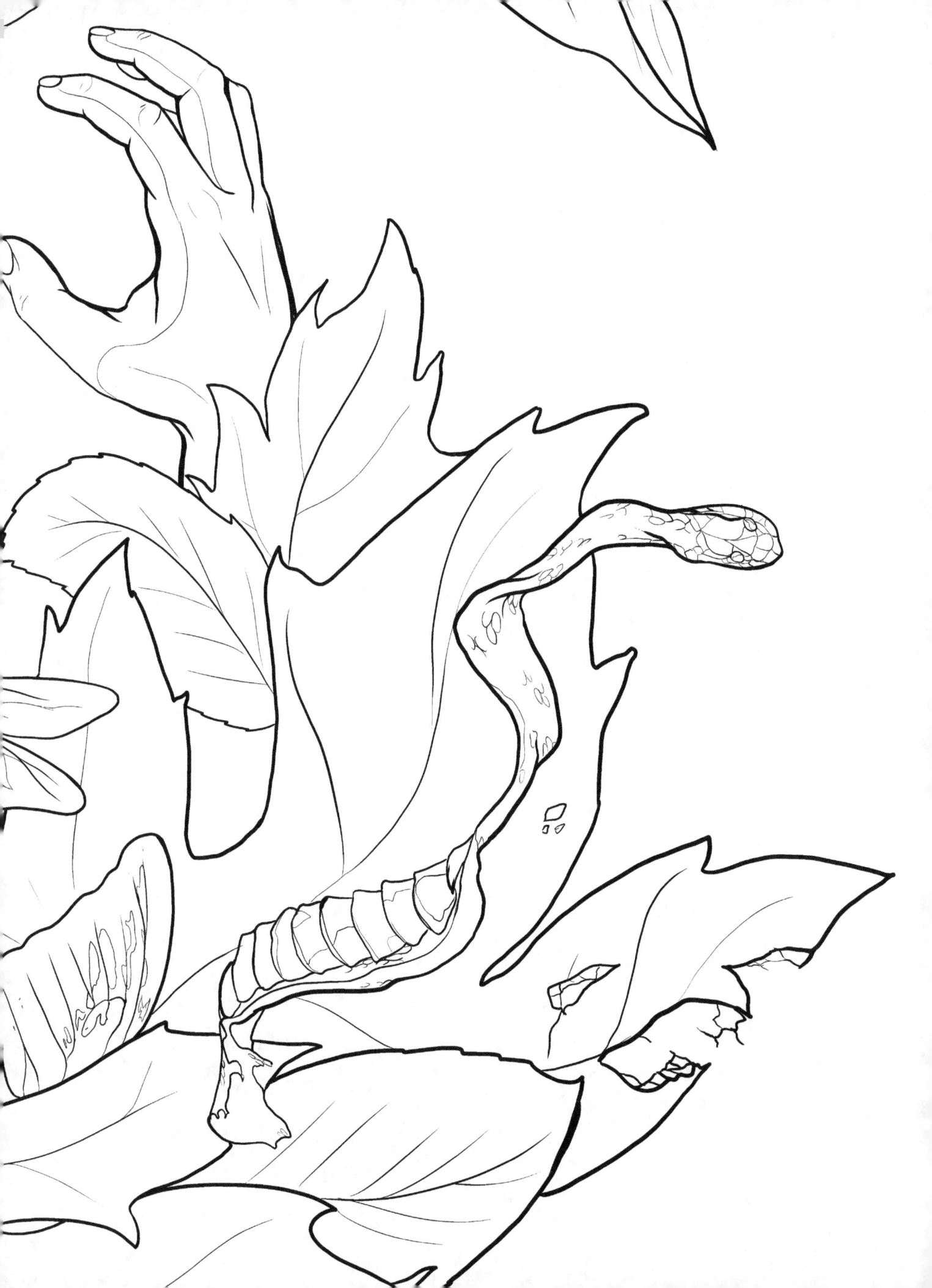

About the author...

Rhea Ewing is an artist and illustrator whose work centers on queer identity, natural history, and Midwest experiences. They've made educational work for Everyday Feminism and Spirit Lake Wellness, illustrated kids books, and are currently working on a 350 page graphic novel about gender in the Midwest called *FINE: a comic about gender.*

By Rhea's reasoning, the value of art is the ability to create connections, question assumptions, and inspire others to do the same.

You can learn more about Rhea's work and how to support future projects at: **RheaEwing.com**

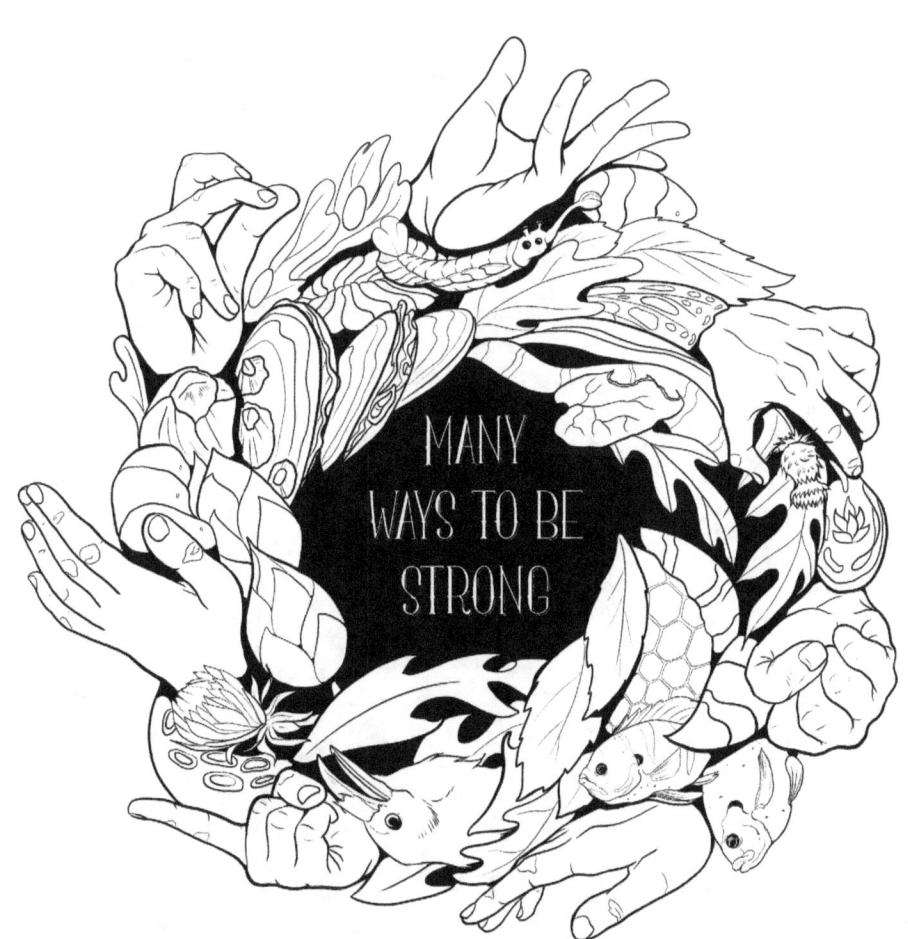

MANY
WAYS TO BE
STRONG

With love and thanks to my family, friends, and above all
my partner, who proofread and edited much of this book.

Liz, you are the loveliest.